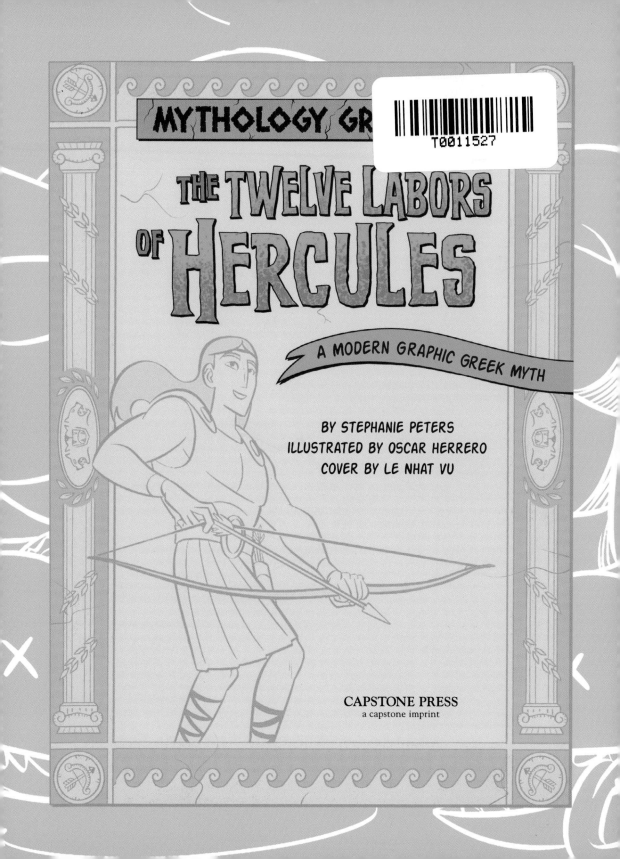

MYTHOLOGY GRE[EK]

THE TWELVE LABORS OF HERCULES

A MODERN GRAPHIC GREEK MYTH

BY STEPHANIE PETERS
ILLUSTRATED BY OSCAR HERRERO
COVER BY LE NHAT VU

CAPSTONE PRESS
a capstone imprint

Published by Capstone Press, an imprint of Capstone
1710 Roe Crest Drive, North Mankato, Minnesota 56003
capstonepub.com

Library of Congress Cataloging-in-Publication Data is available on the Library of Congress website.

ISBN: 9781669050933 (hardcover)
ISBN: 9781669050889 (paperback)
ISBN: 9781669050896 (ebook PDF)

Summary: Hercules is the ultimate Greek hero—just ask him. But to redeem himself, he must complete a series of dangerous missions given to him by his scheming cousin. It's up to Hercules to prove his strength and wit. Find out if he succeeds in this modern, graphic retelling of a classic Greek myth.

Editorial Credits
Editor: Alison Deering; Designer: Jaime Willems;
Production Specialist: Whitney Schaefer

All internet sites appearing in back matter were available and accurate when this book was sent to press.

Printed and bound in the USA. PO#5425

TABLE OF CONTENTS

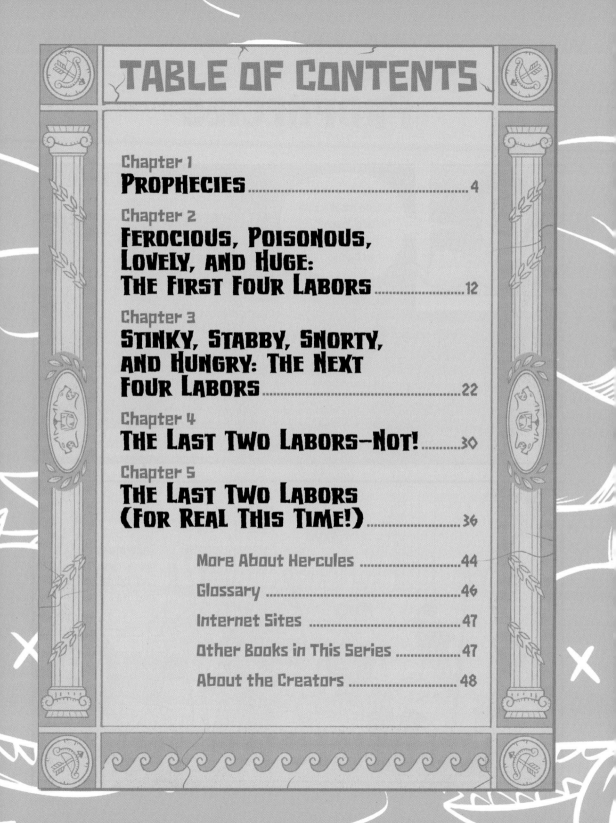

CHAPTER 1

PROPHECIES

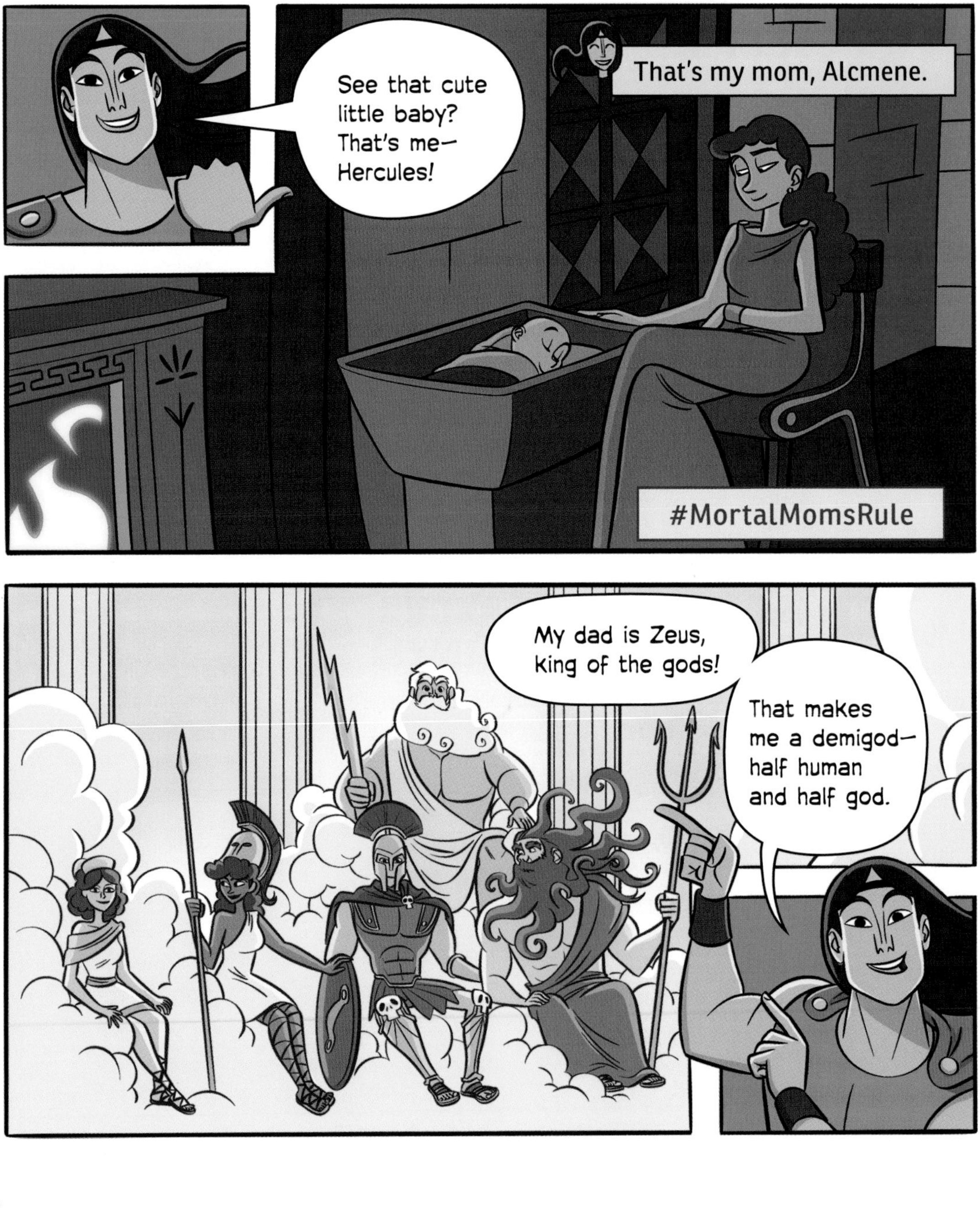
See that cute little baby? That's me—Hercules!
That's my mom, Alcmene.
#MortalMomsRule
My dad is Zeus, King of the gods!
That makes me a demigod—half human and half god.

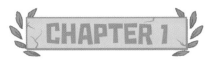

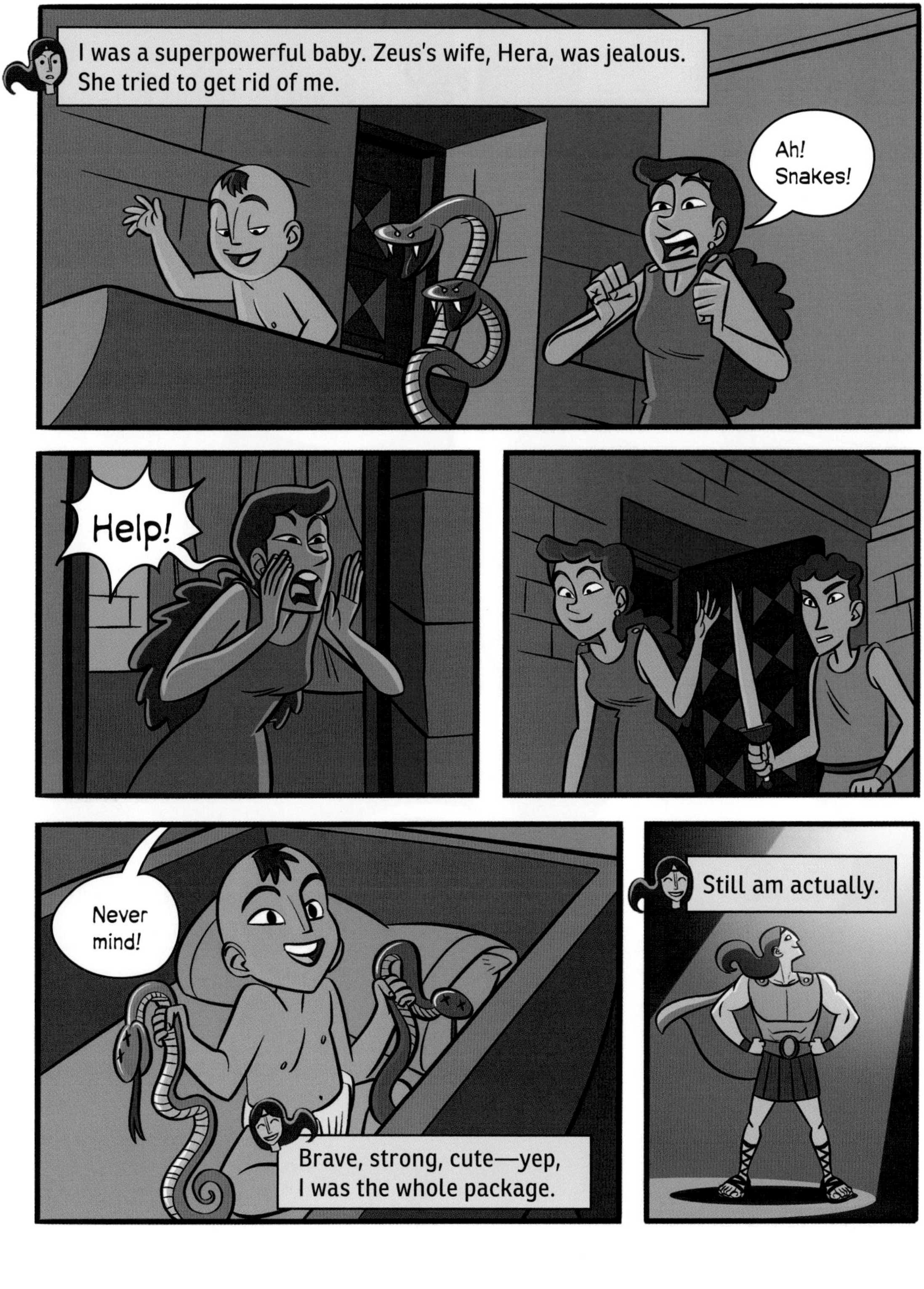
I was a superpowerful baby. Zeus's wife, Hera, was jealous. She tried to get rid of me.
Ah! Snakes!
Help!
Never mind!
Brave, strong, cute—yep, I was the whole package.
Still am actually.

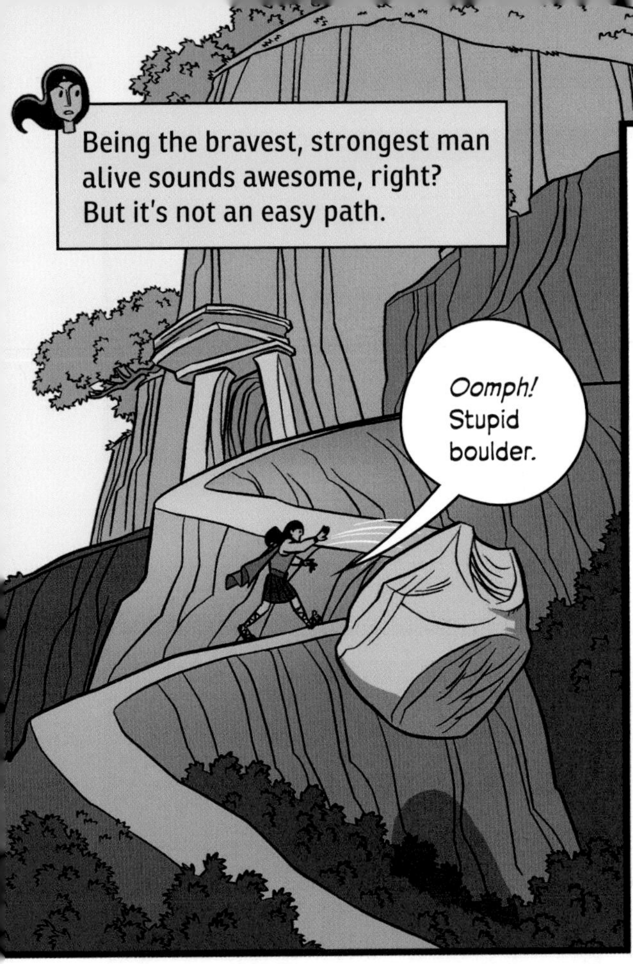
Being the bravest, strongest man alive sounds awesome, right? But it's not an easy path.
Oomph! Stupid boulder.

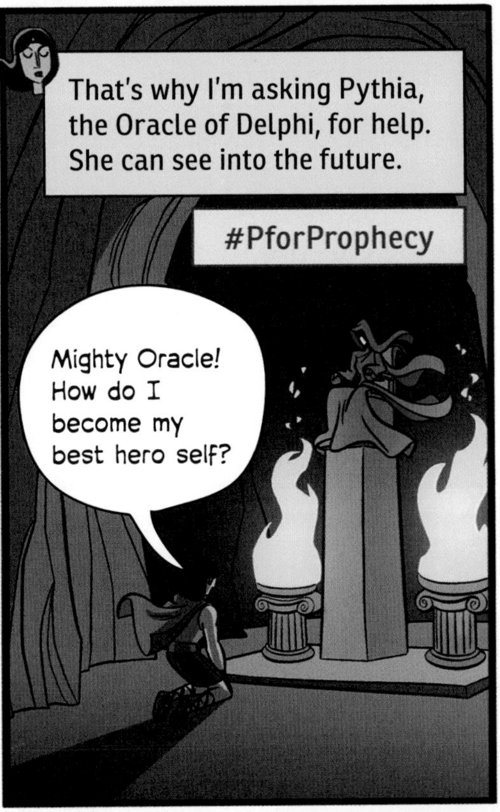
That's why I'm asking Pythia, the Oracle of Delphi, for help. She can see into the future.
#PforProphecy
Mighty Oracle! How do I become my best hero self?

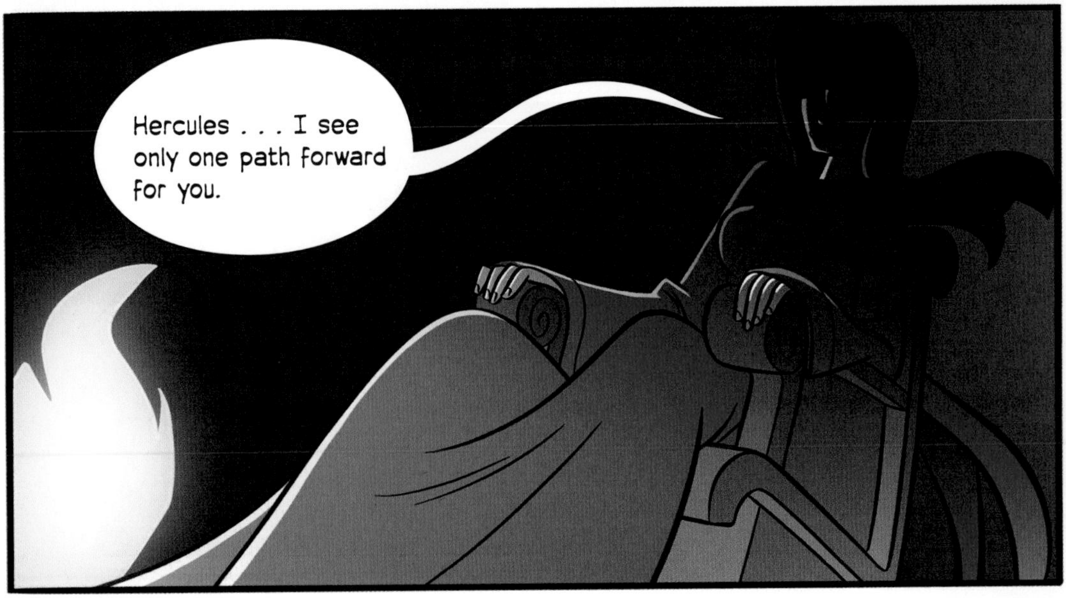
Hercules . . . I see only one path forward for you.

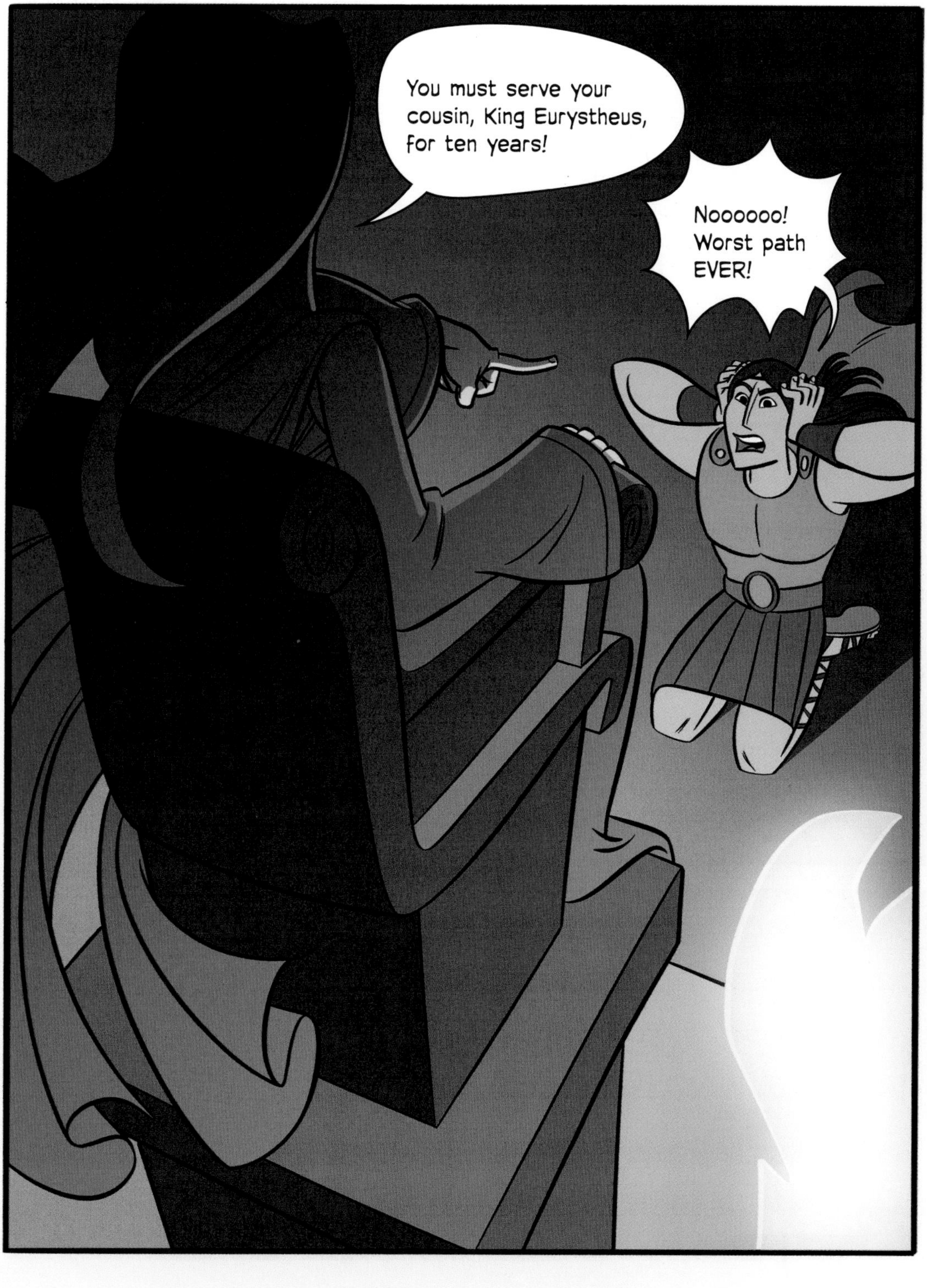
You must serve your cousin, King Eurystheus, for ten years!
Noooooo! Worst path EVER!

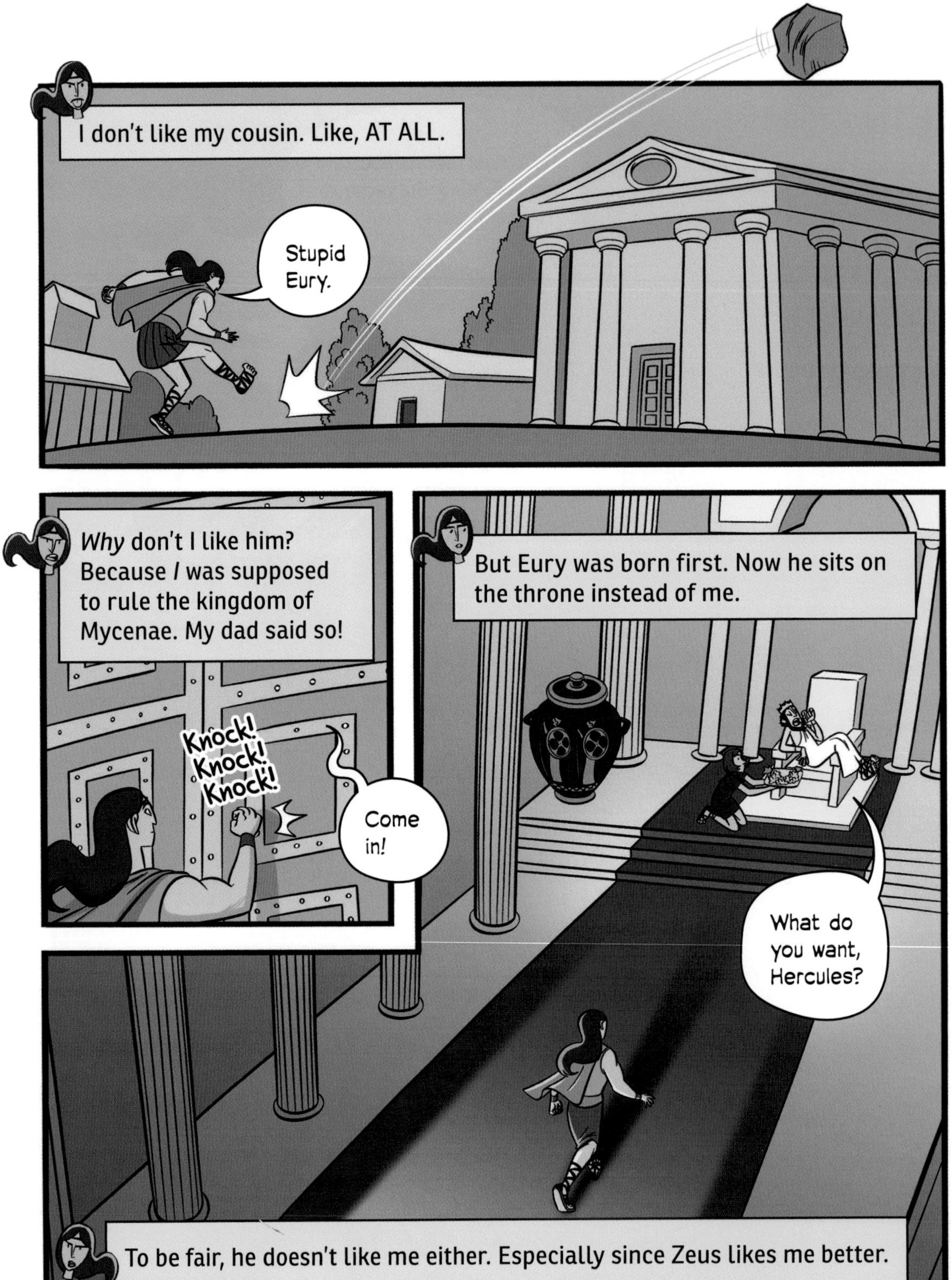
I don't like my cousin. Like, AT ALL.
Stupid Eury.
Why don't I like him? Because *I* was supposed to rule the kingdom of Mycenae. My dad said so!
Knock! Knock! Knock!
Come in!
But Eury was born first. Now he sits on the throne instead of me.
What do you want, Hercules?
To be fair, he doesn't like me either. Especially since Zeus likes me better.

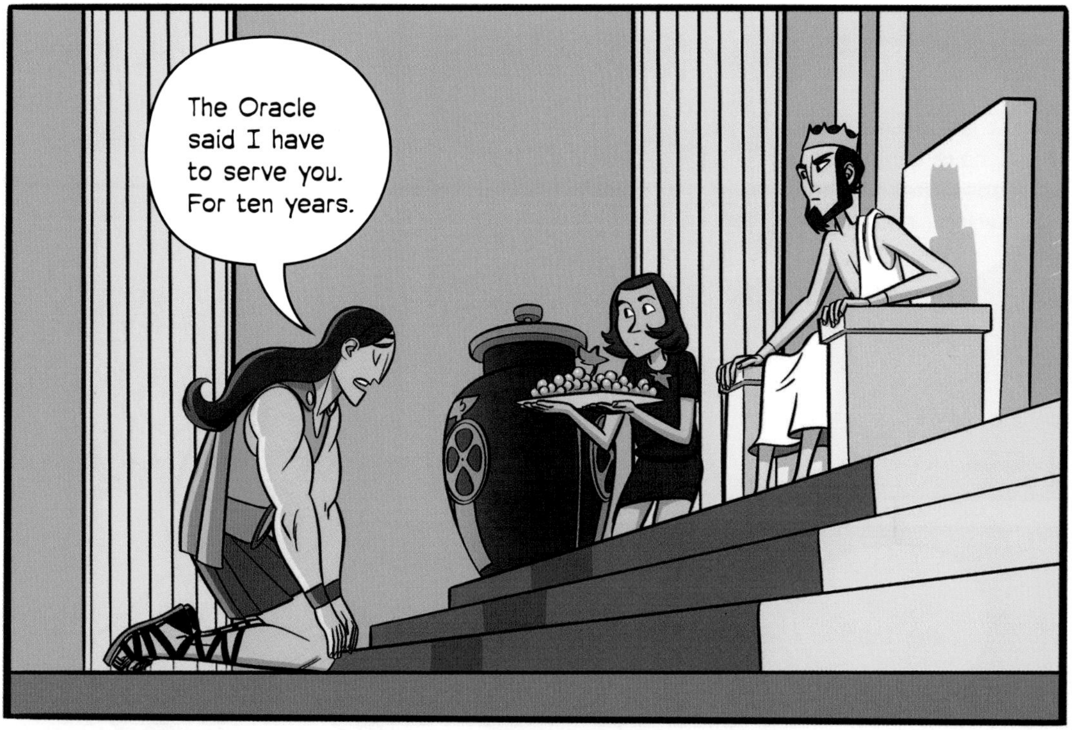
The Oracle said I have to serve you. For ten years.

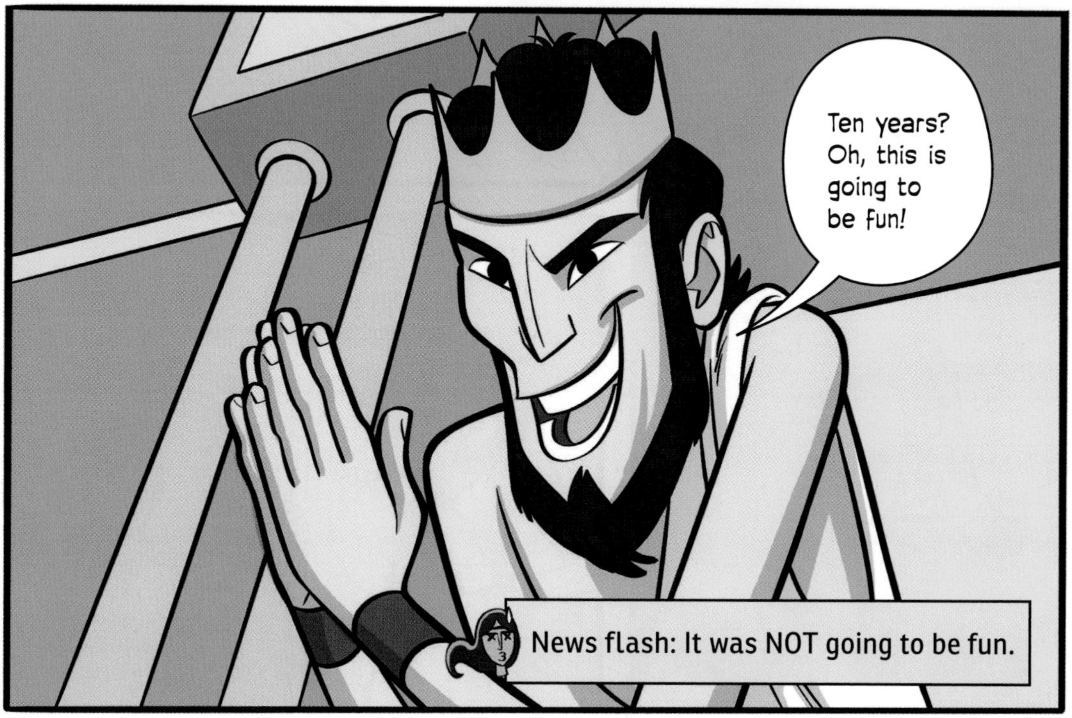
Ten years? Oh, this is going to be fun!
News flash: It was NOT going to be fun.

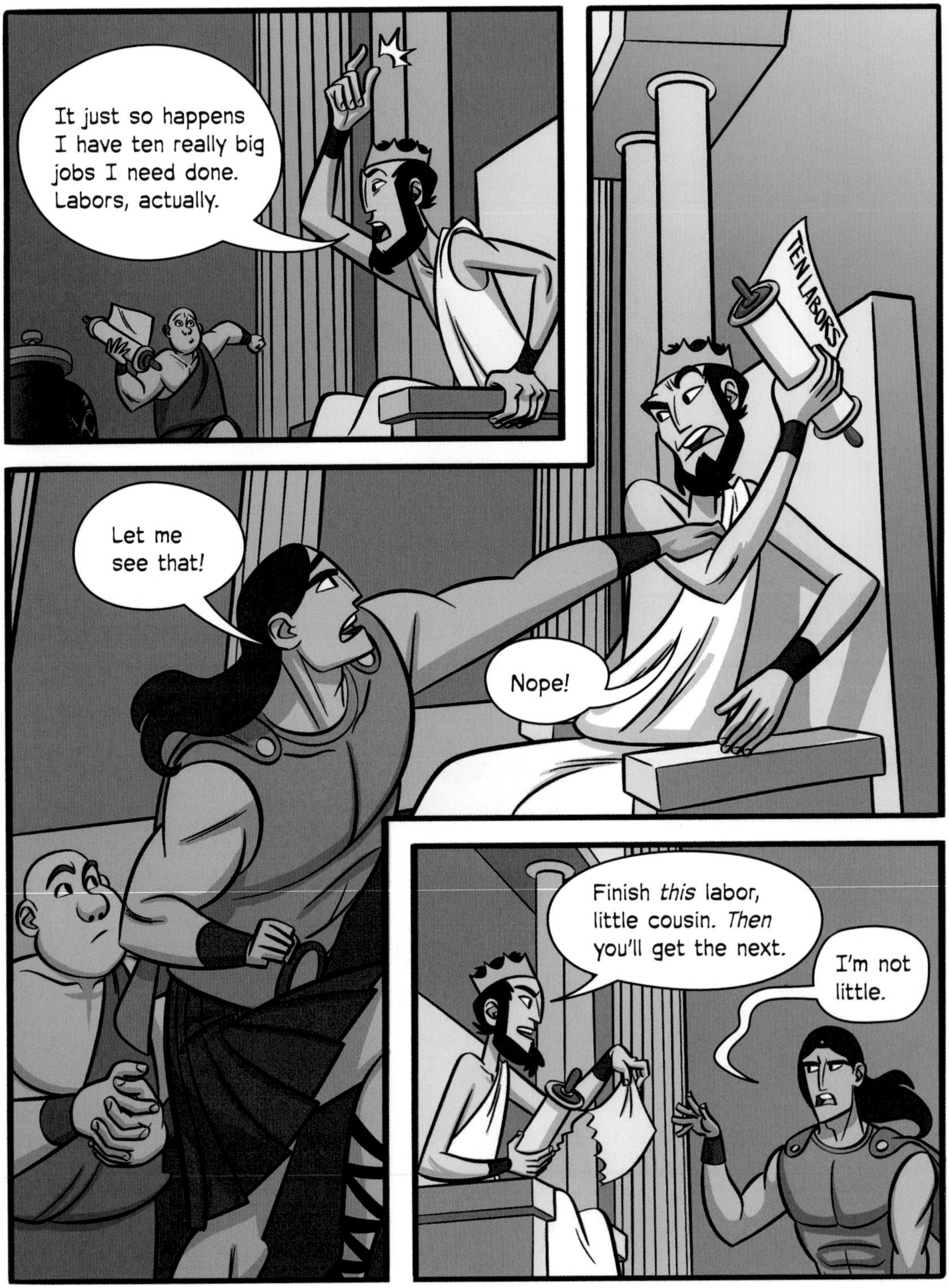

It just so happens I have ten really big jobs I need done. Labors, actually.
TEN LABORS
Let me see that!
Nope!
Finish *this* labor, little cousin. *Then* you'll get the next.
I'm not little.

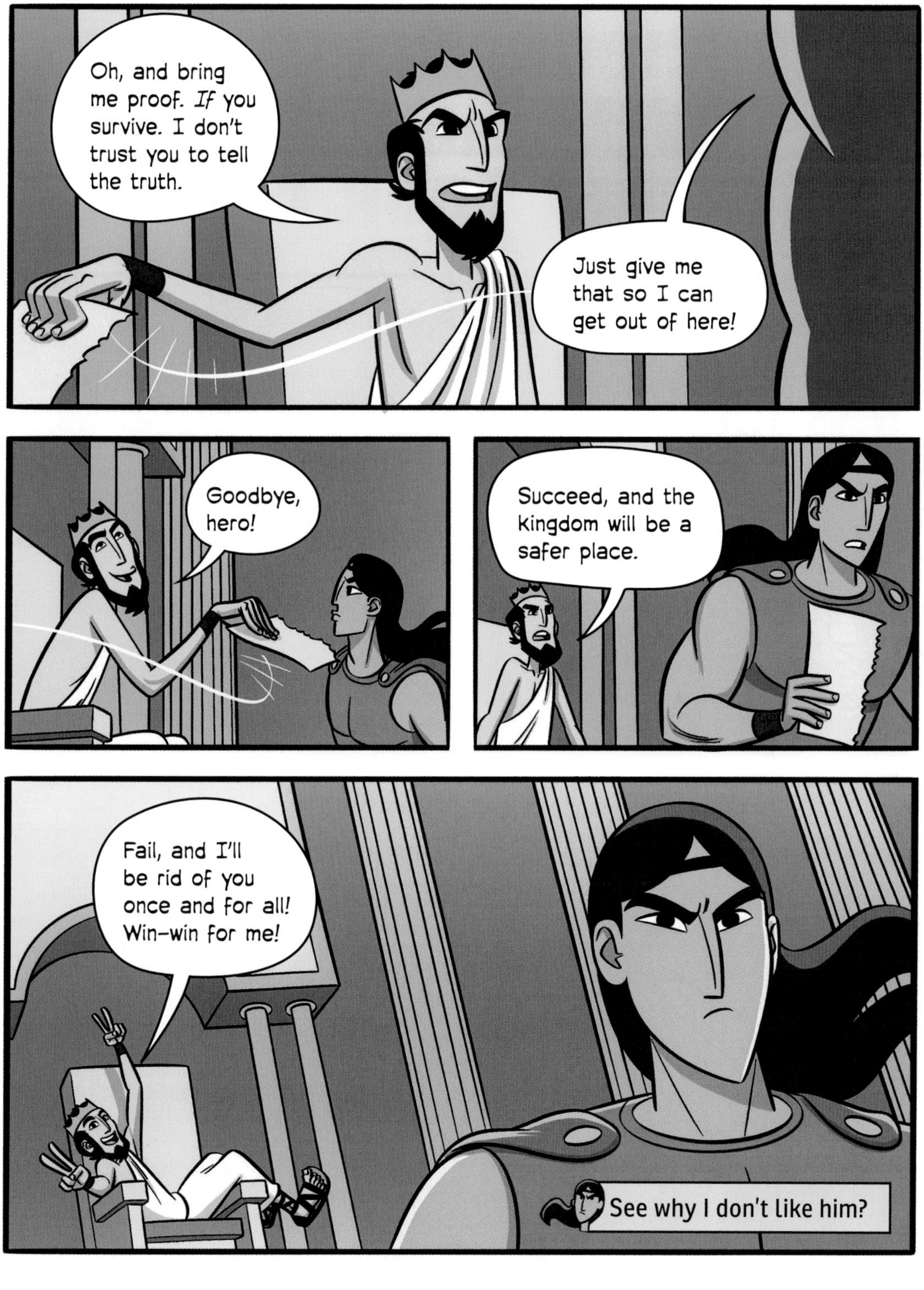
Oh, and bring me proof. *If* you survive. I don't trust you to tell the truth.
Just give me that so I can get out of here!
Goodbye, hero!
Succeed, and the kingdom will be a safer place.
Fail, and I'll be rid of you once and for all! Win-win for me!
See why I don't like him?

CHAPTER 2

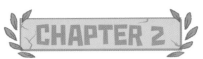

FEROCIOUS, POISONOUS, LOVELY, AND HUGE: THE FIRST FOUR LABORS

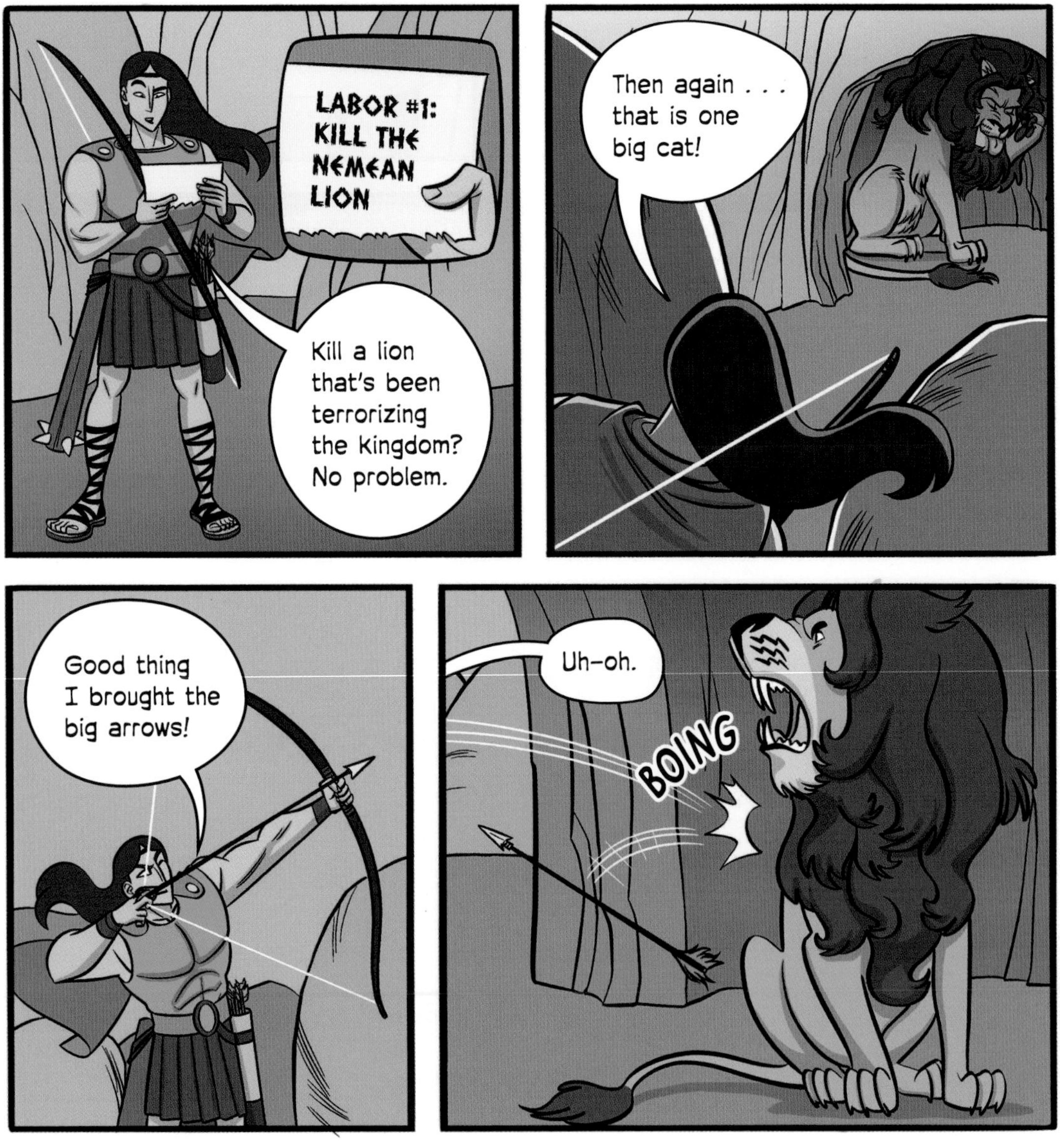
LABOR #1: KILL THE NEMEAN LION
Kill a lion that's been terrorizing the kingdom? No problem.
Then again . . . that is one big cat!
Good thing I brought the big arrows!
Uh-oh.
BOING

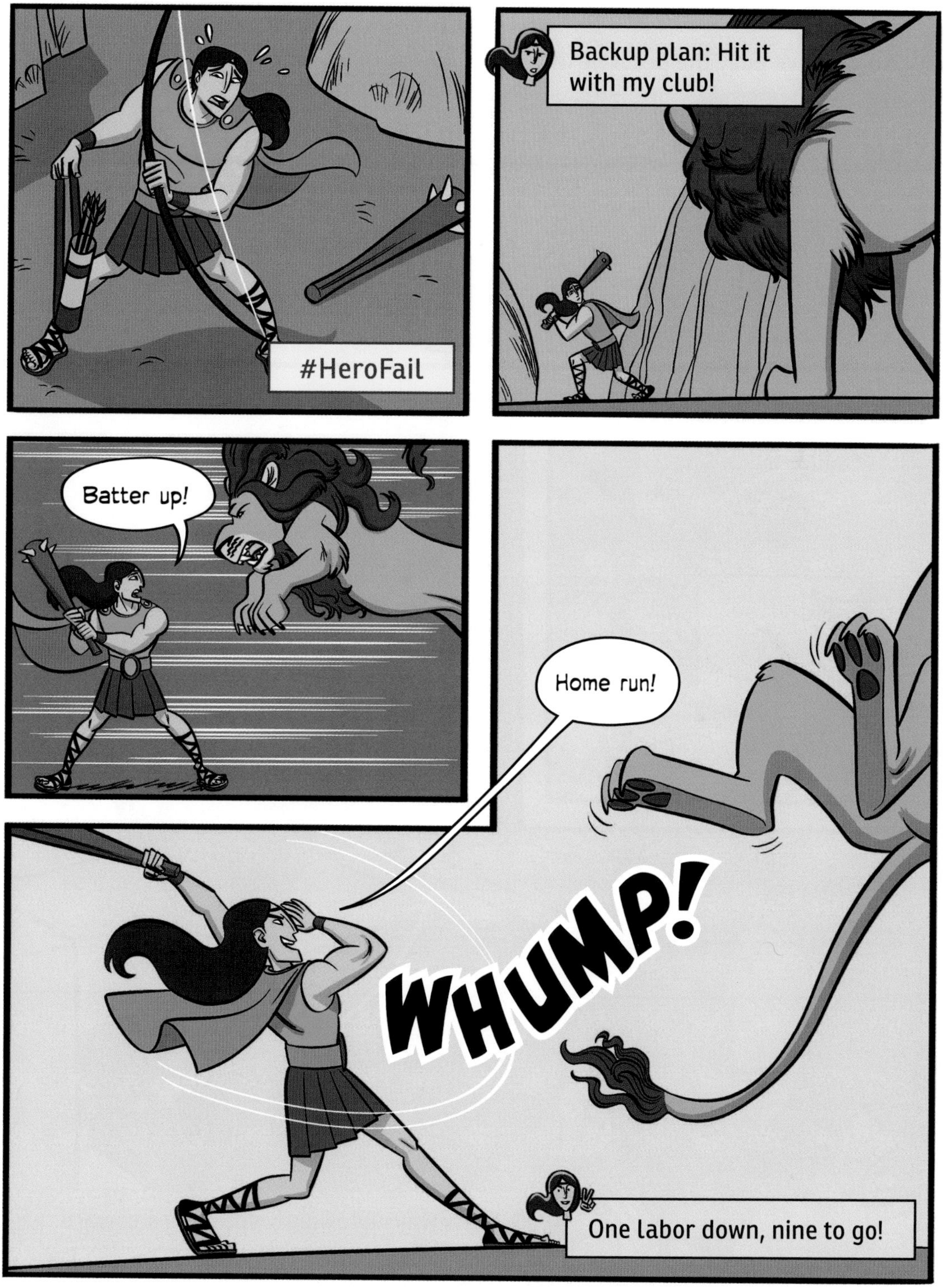
#HeroFail
Backup plan: Hit it with my club!
Batter up!
Home run!
WHUMP!
One labor down, nine to go!

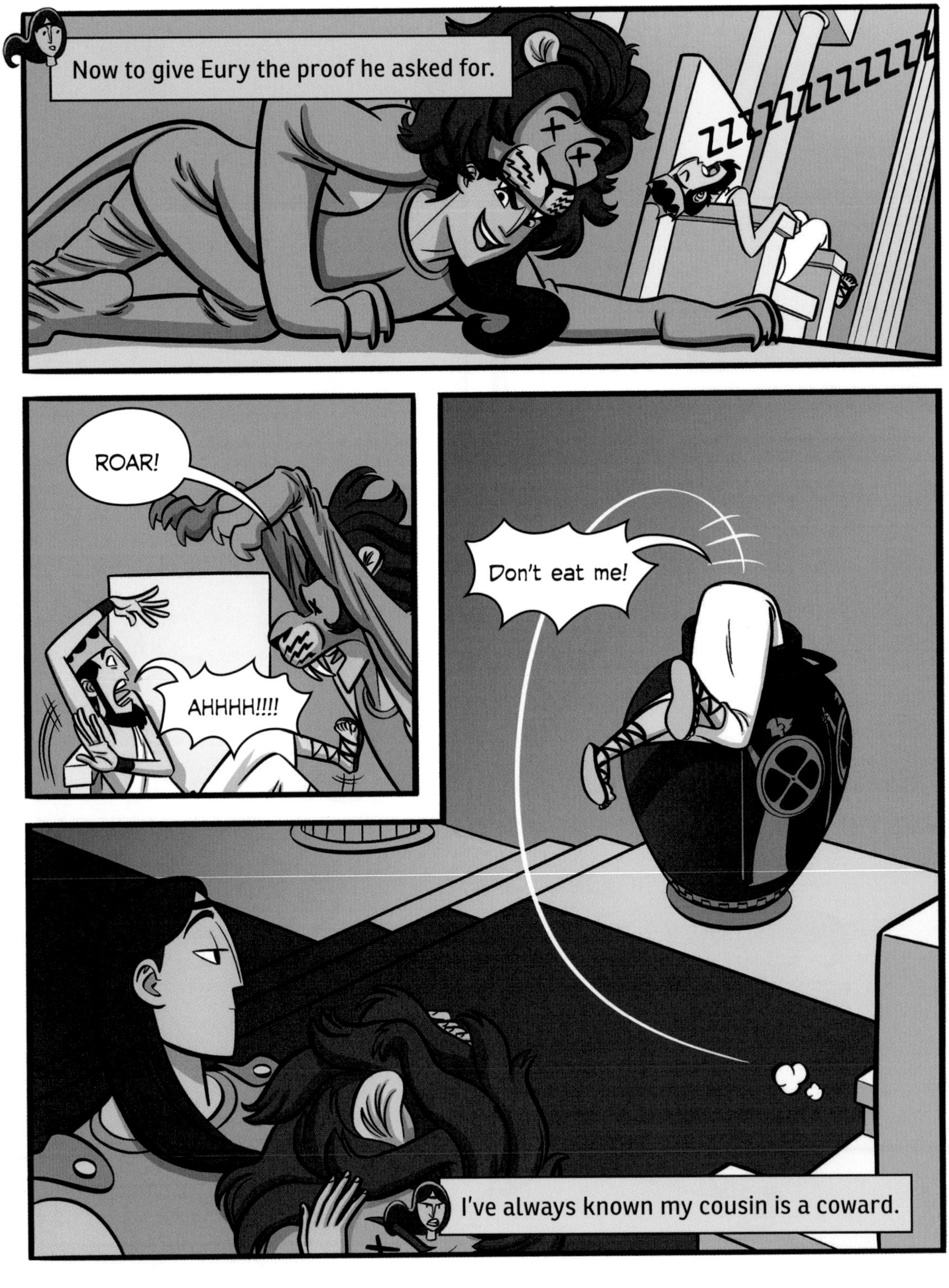
Now to give Eury the proof he asked for.
ZZZZZZZZZZZZ
ROAR!
AHHHH!!!!
Don't eat me!
I've always known my cousin is a coward.

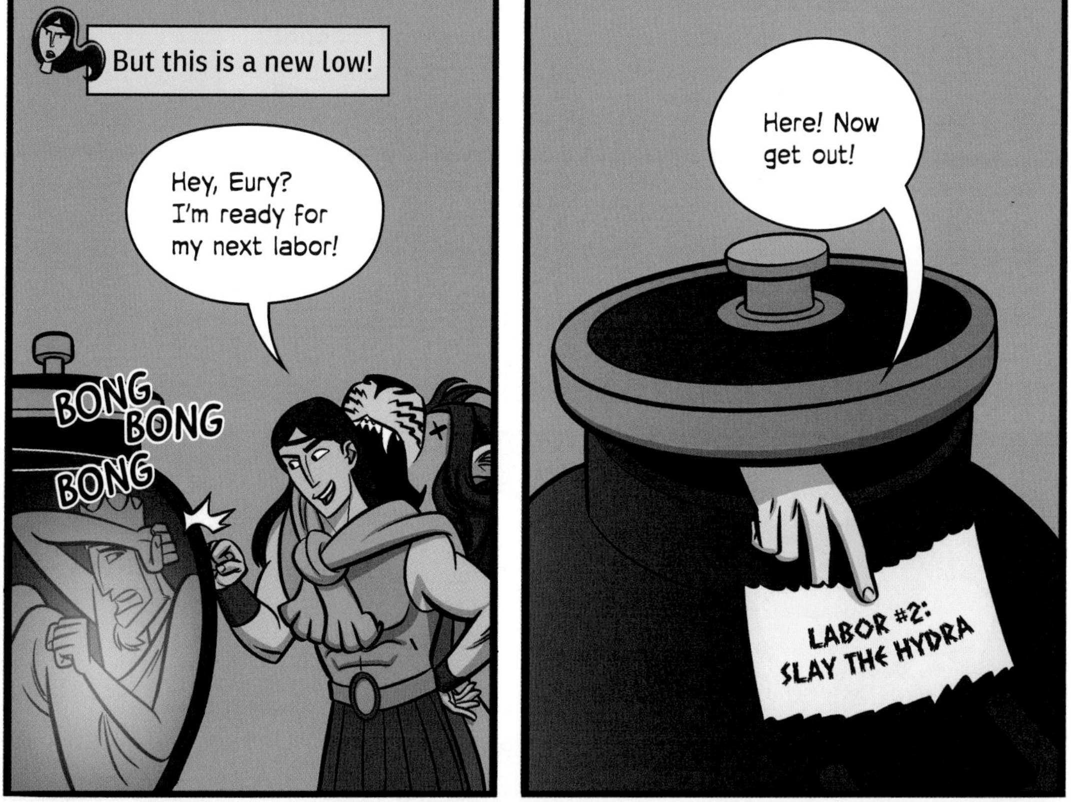
But this is a new low!
Hey, Eury? I'm ready for my next labor!
BONG BONG BONG
Here! Now get out!
LABOR #2: SLAY THE HYDRA

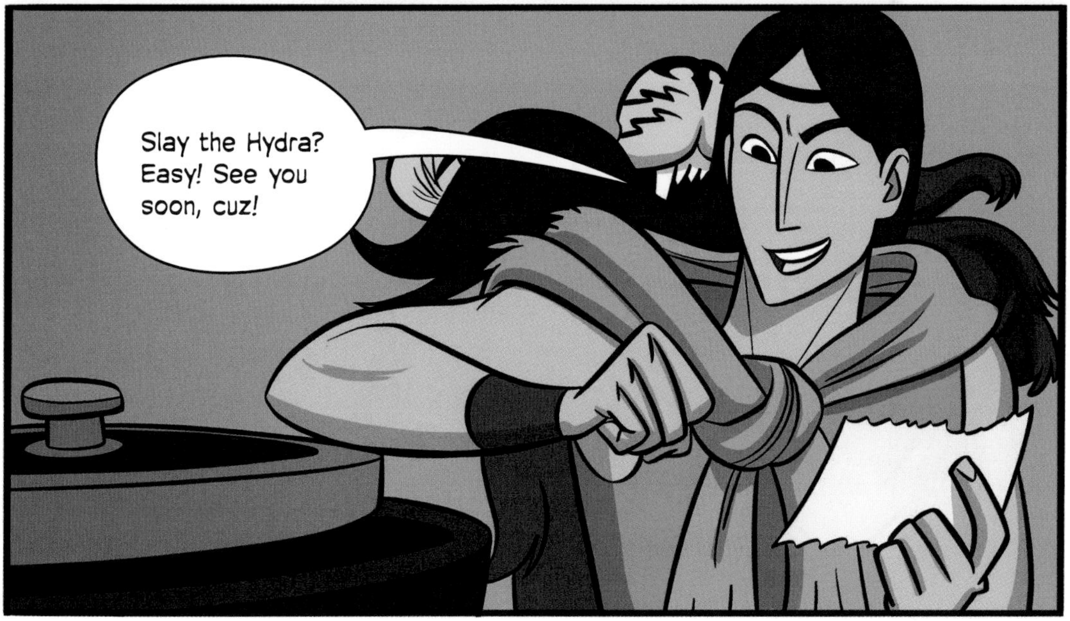
Slay the Hydra? Easy! See you soon, cuz!

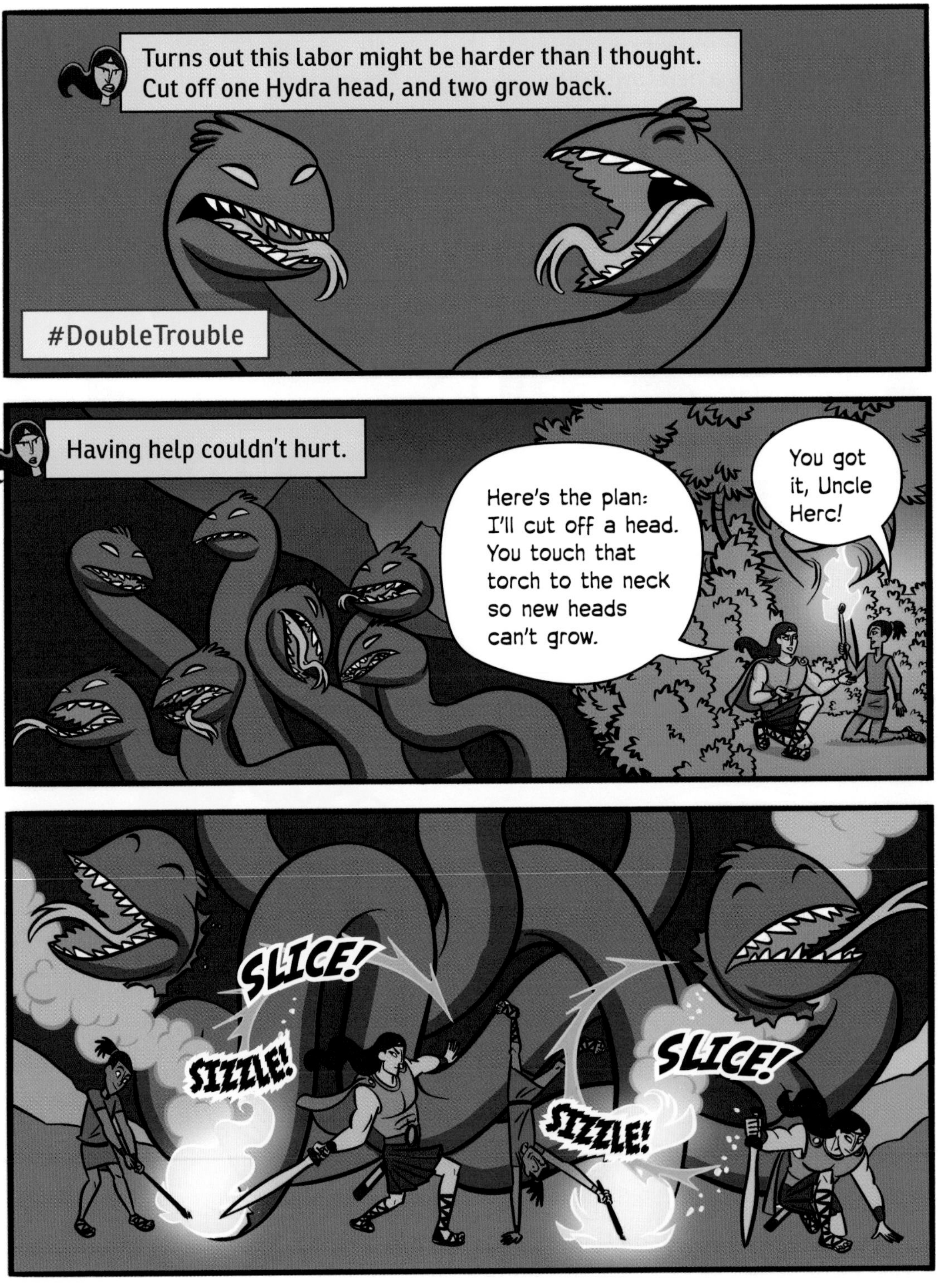
Turns out this labor might be harder than I thought. Cut off one Hydra head, and two grow back.
#DoubleTrouble
Having help couldn't hurt.
Here's the plan: I'll cut off a head. You touch that torch to the neck so new heads can't grow.
You got it, Uncle Herc!
SLICE!
SIZZLE!
SIZZLE!
SLICE!

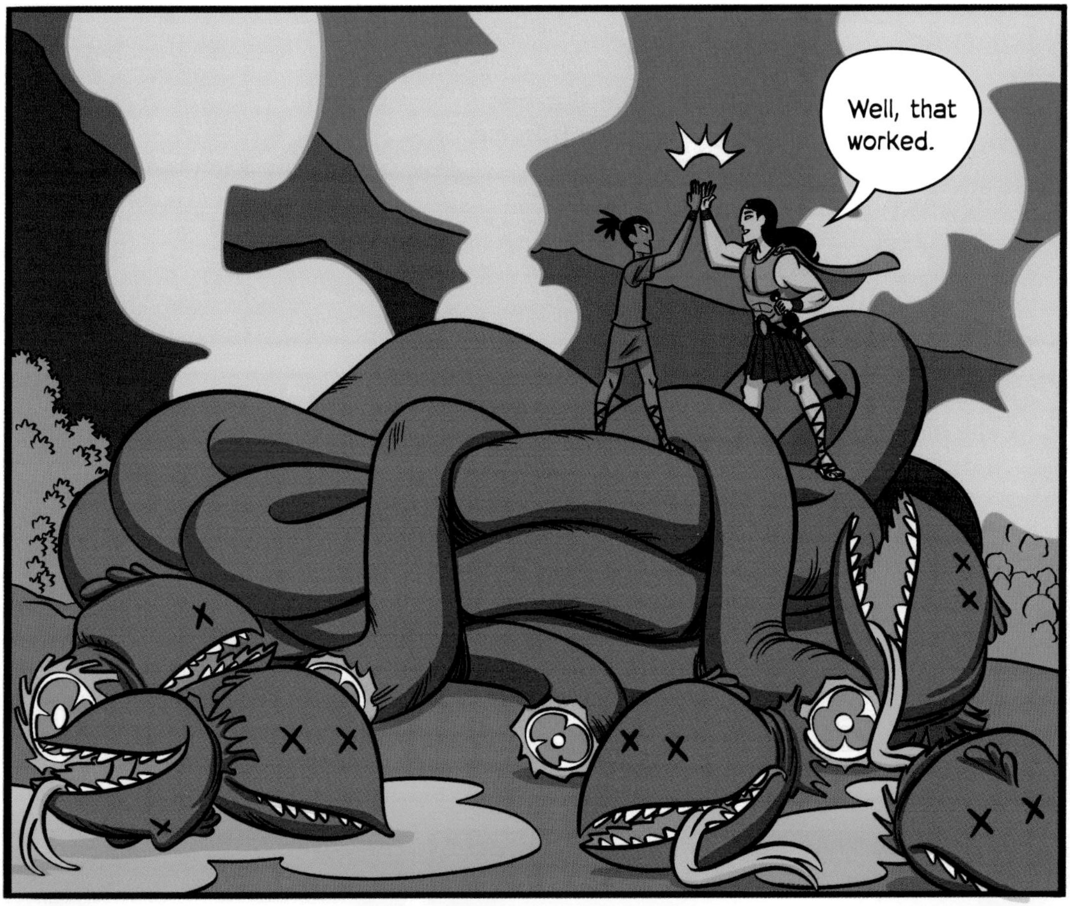
Well, that worked.

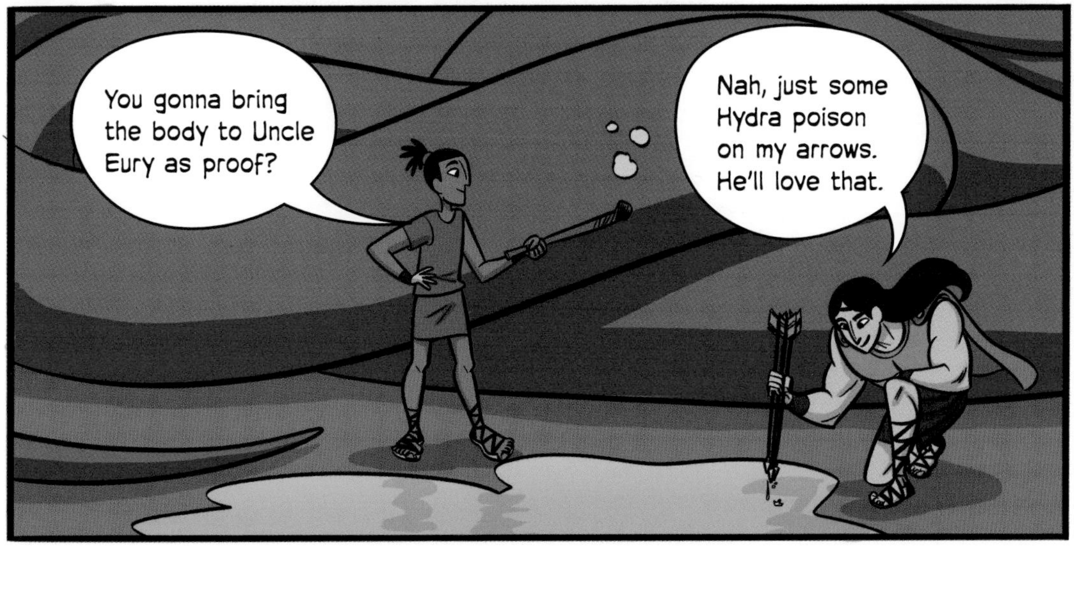
You gonna bring the body to Uncle Eury as proof?
Nah, just some Hydra poison on my arrows. He'll love that.

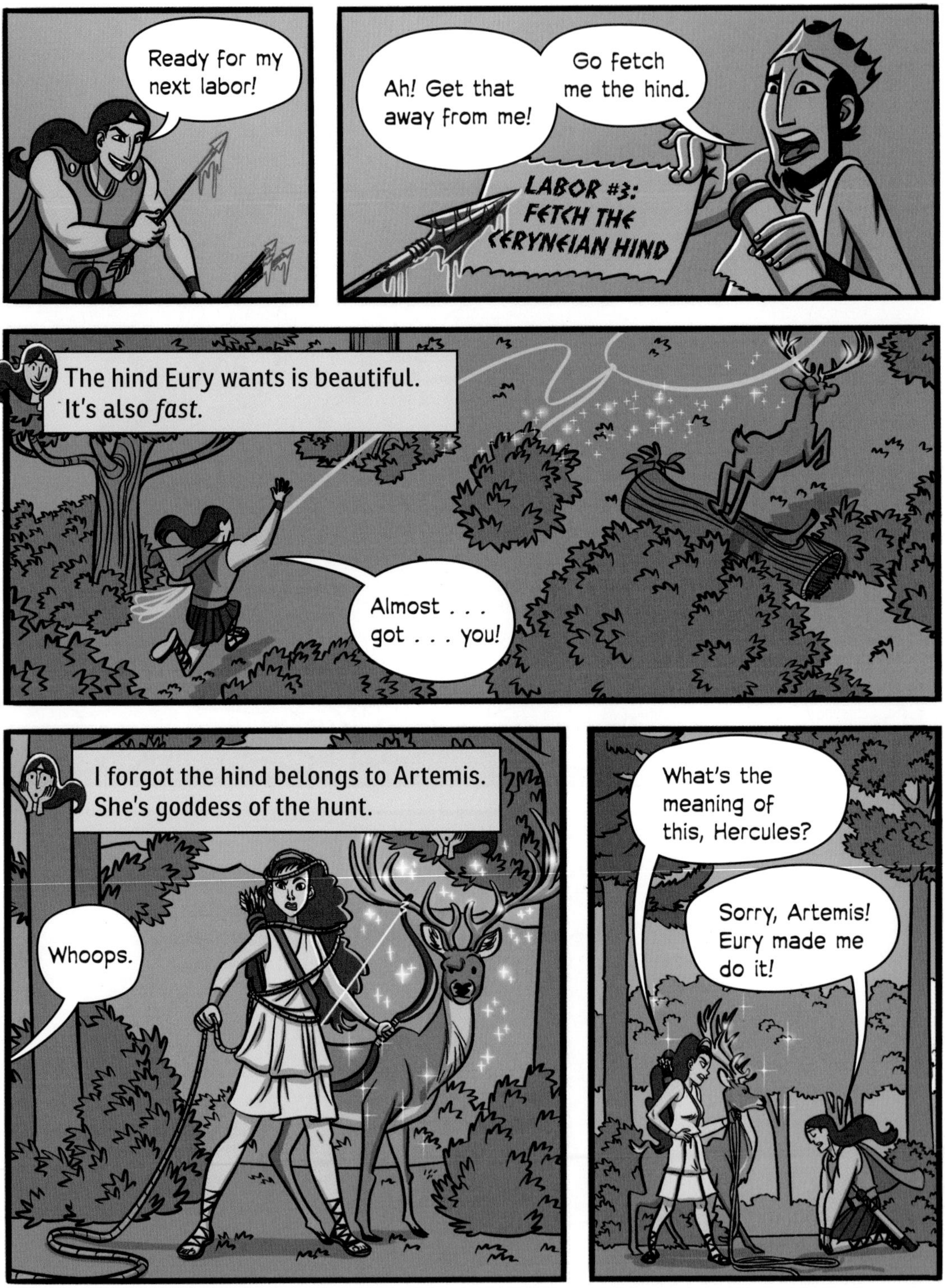

Ready for my next labor!
Ah! Get that away from me!
Go fetch me the hind.
LABOR #3: FETCH THE CERYNEIAN HIND
The hind Eury wants is beautiful. It's also *fast*.
Almost . . . got . . . you!
I forgot the hind belongs to Artemis. She's goddess of the hunt.
Whoops.
What's the meaning of this, Hercules?
Sorry, Artemis! Eury made me do it!

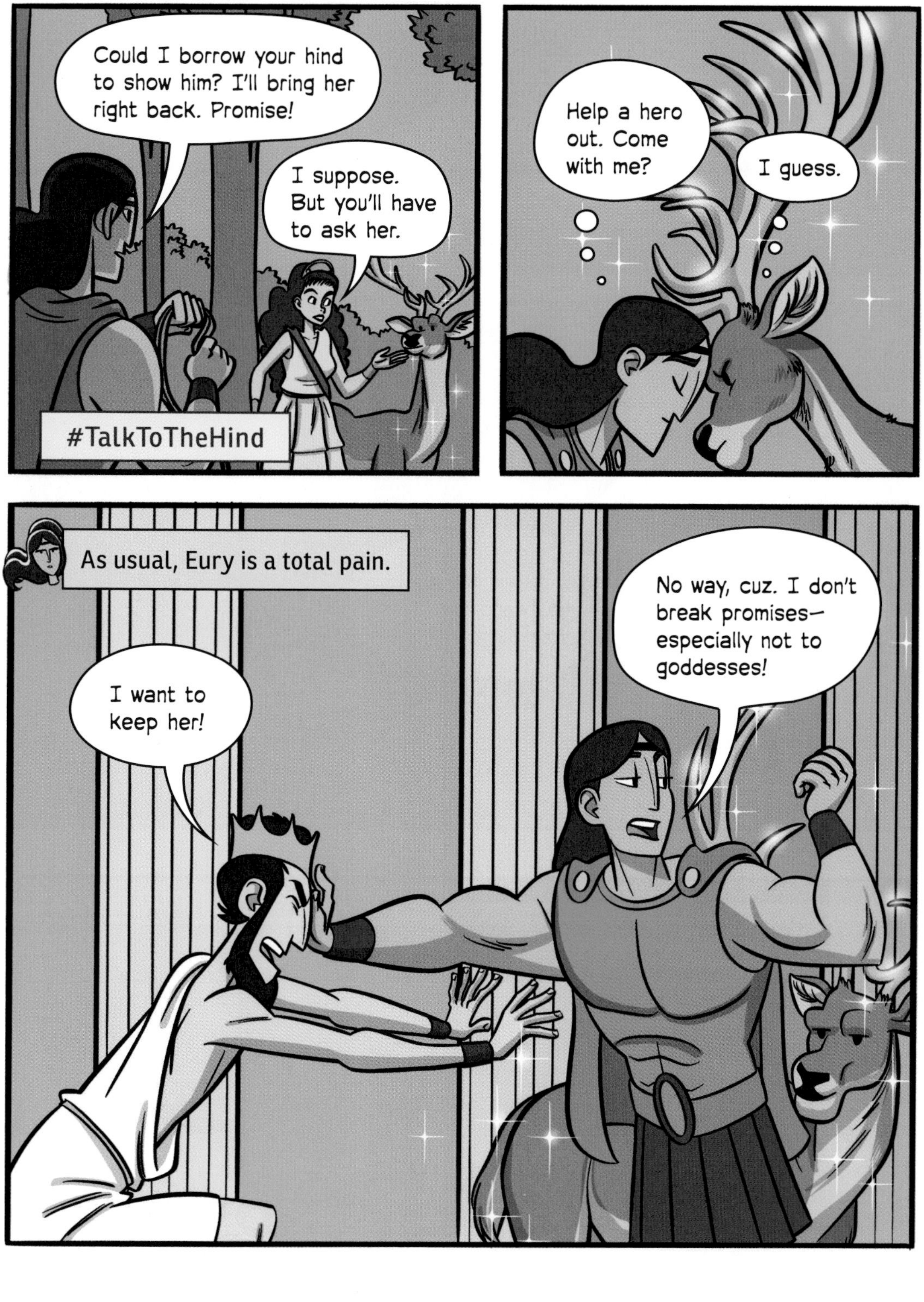
Could I borrow your hind to show him? I'll bring her right back. Promise!
I suppose. But you'll have to ask her.
#TalkToTheHind
Help a hero out. Come with me?
I guess.
As usual, Eury is a total pain.
I want to keep her!
No way, cuz. I don't break promises— especially not to goddesses!

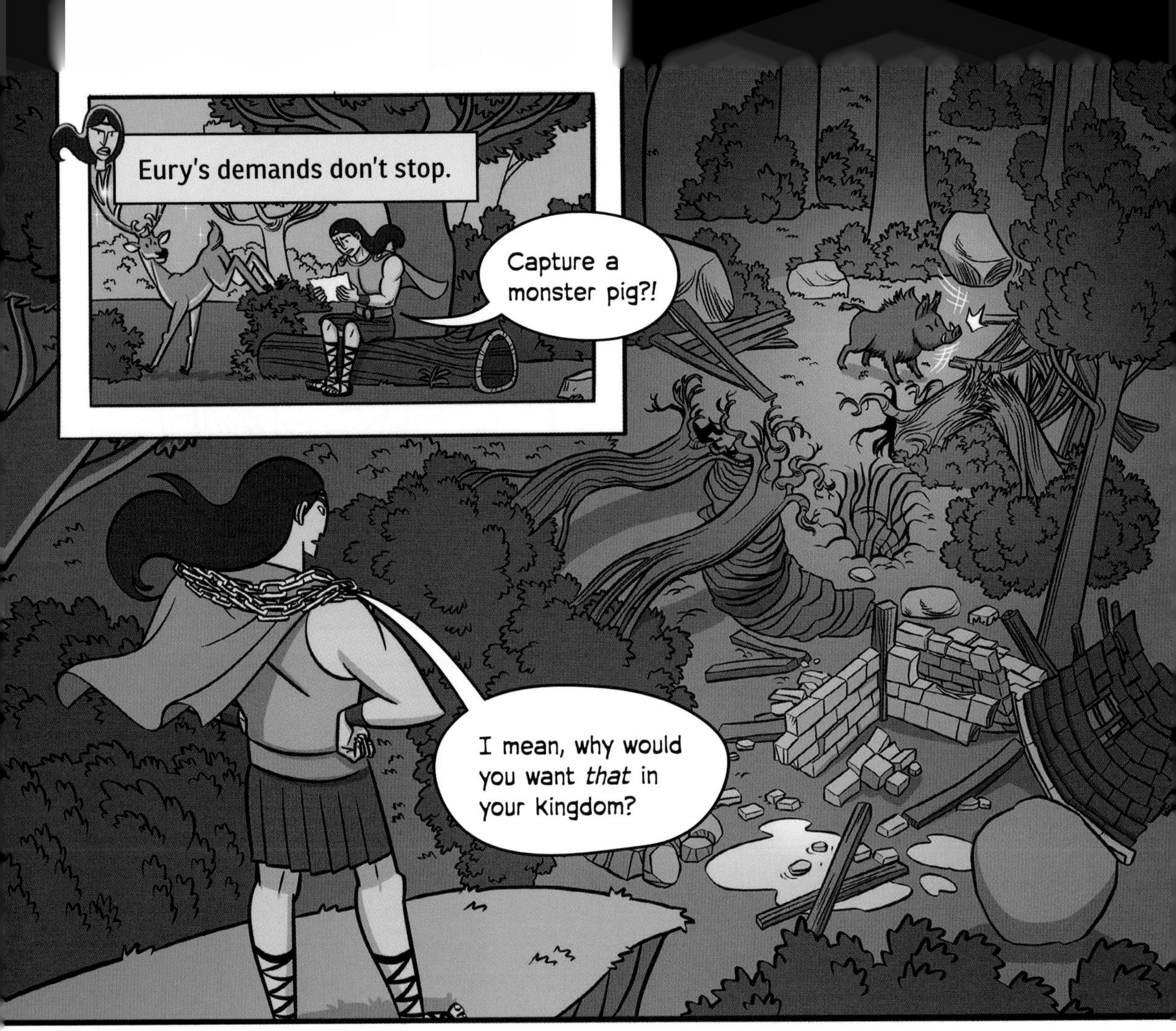
Eury's demands don't stop.
Capture a monster pig?!
I mean, why would you want *that* in your kingdom?

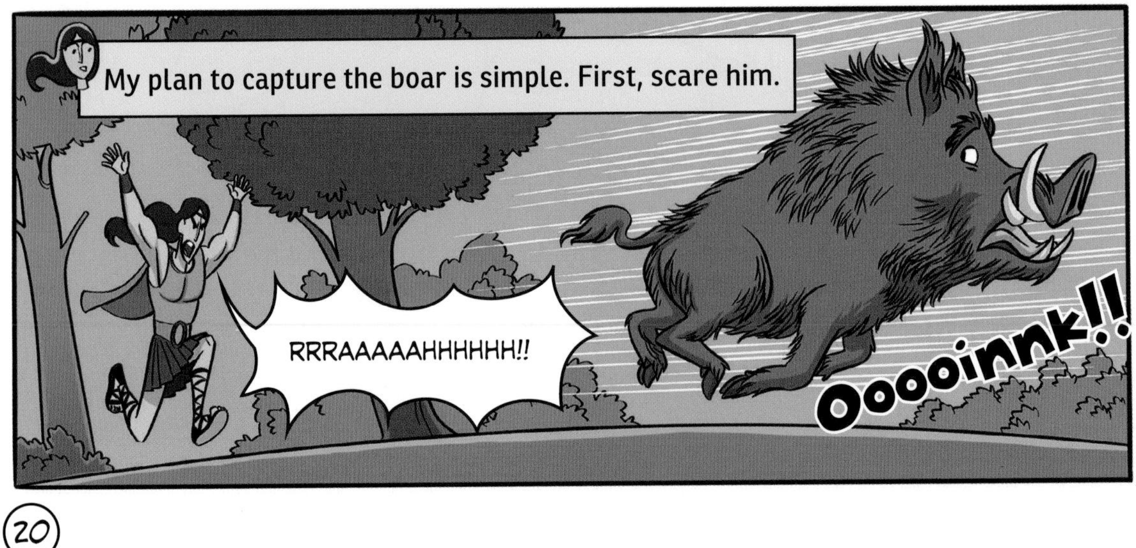
My plan to capture the boar is simple. First, scare him.
RRRAAAAAHHHHHH!!
Ooooinnk!!

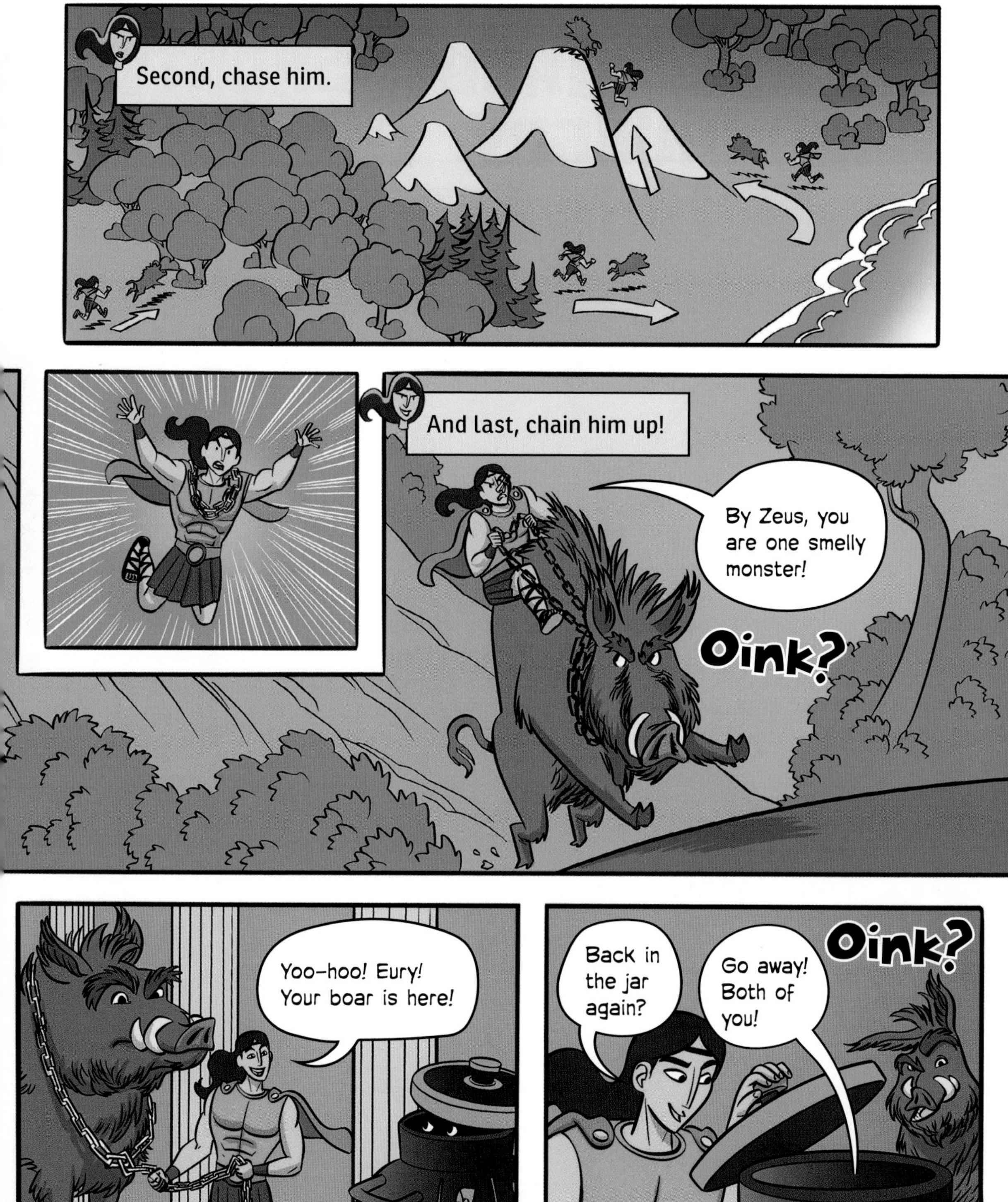
Second, chase him.
And last, chain him up!
By Zeus, you are one smelly monster!
Oink?
Yoo-hoo! Eury! Your boar is here!
Back in the jar again?
Go away! Both of you!
Oink?

CHAPTER 3

STINKY, STABBY, SNORTY, AND HUNGRY: THE NEXT FOUR LABORS

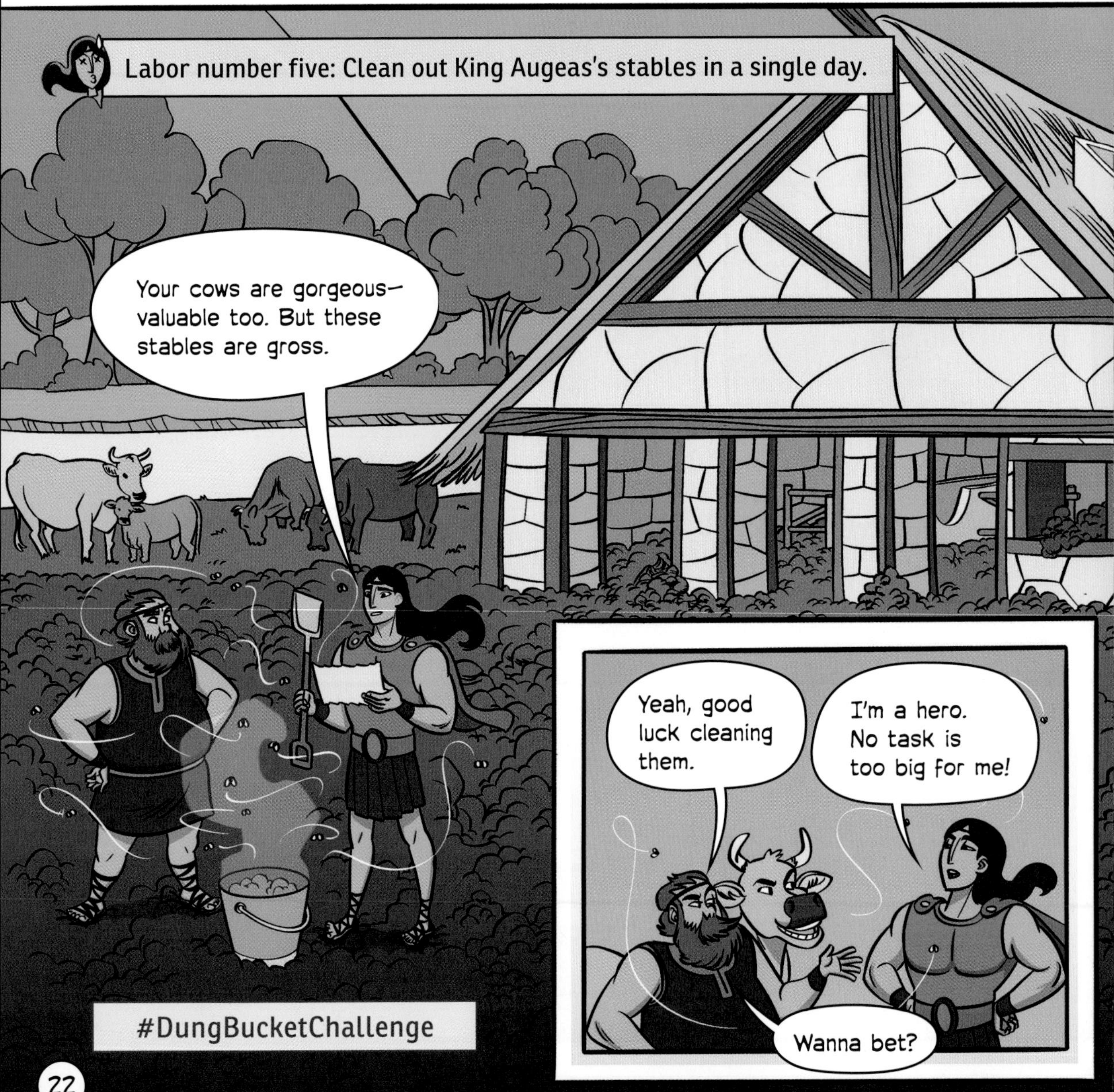

Labor number five: Clean out King Augeas's stables in a single day.
Your cows are gorgeous—valuable too. But these stables are gross.
#DungBucketChallenge
Yeah, good luck cleaning them.
I'm a hero. No task is too big for me!
Wanna bet?

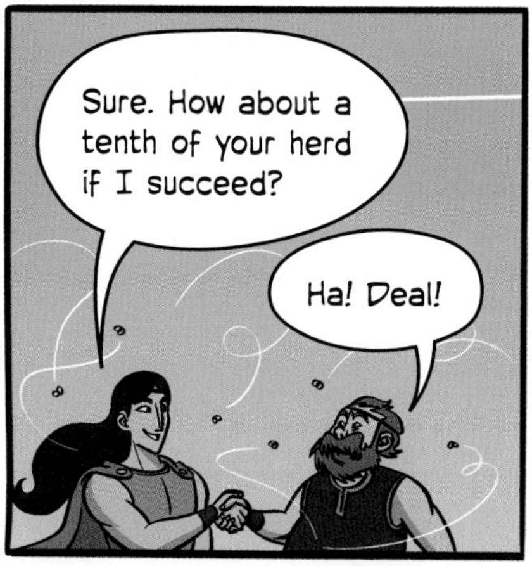
Sure. How about a tenth of your herd if I succeed?
Ha! Deal!
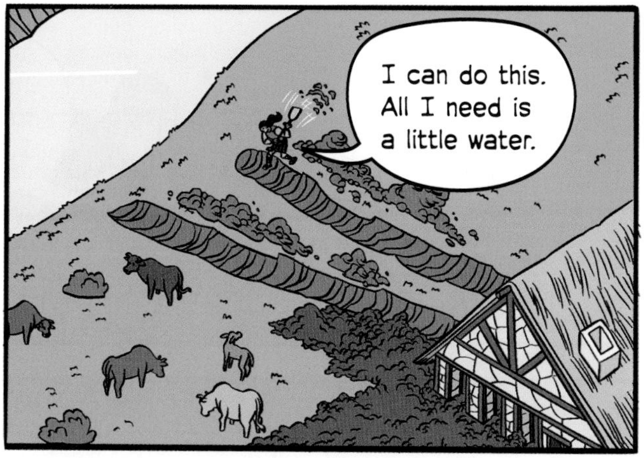
I can do this. All I need is a little water.
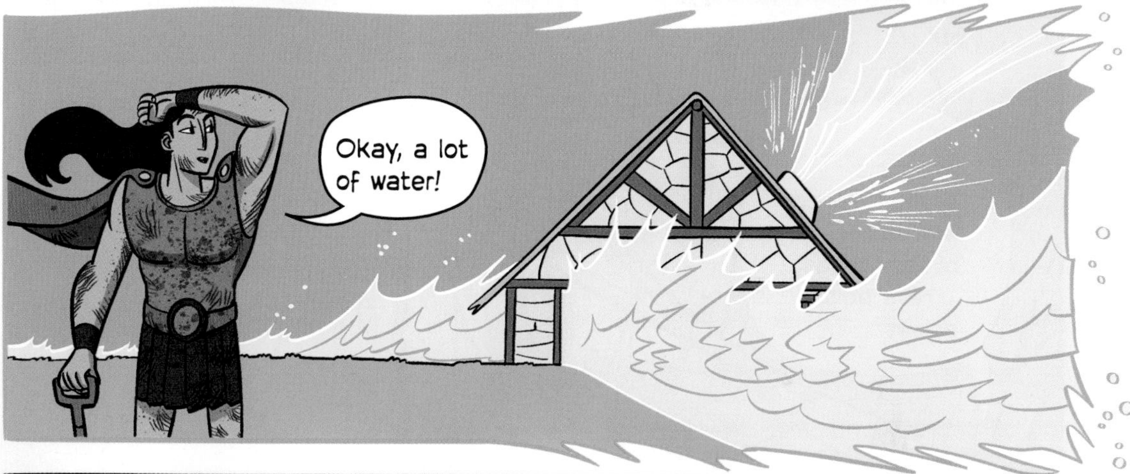
Okay, a lot of water!
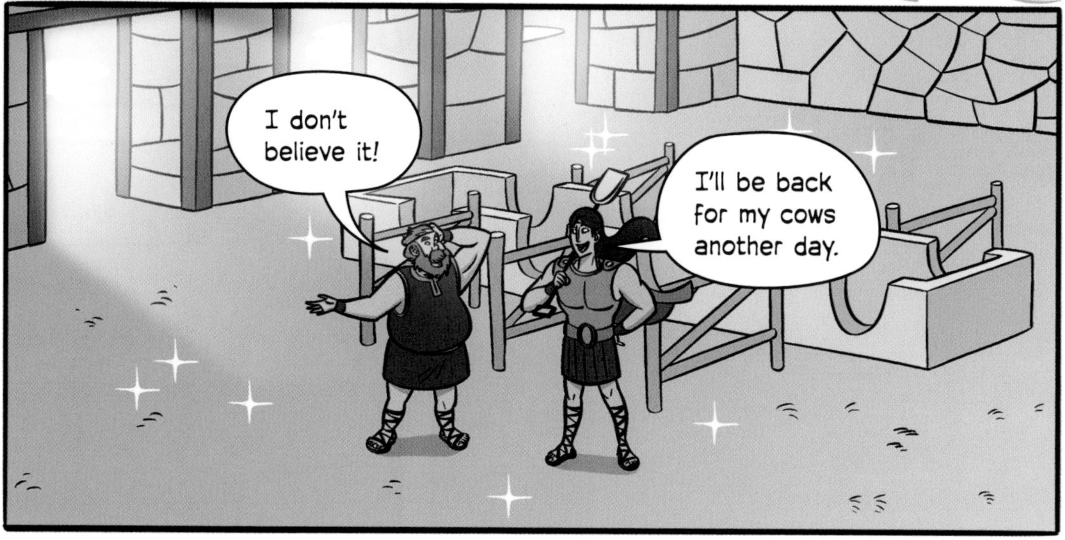
I don't believe it!
I'll be back for my cows another day.

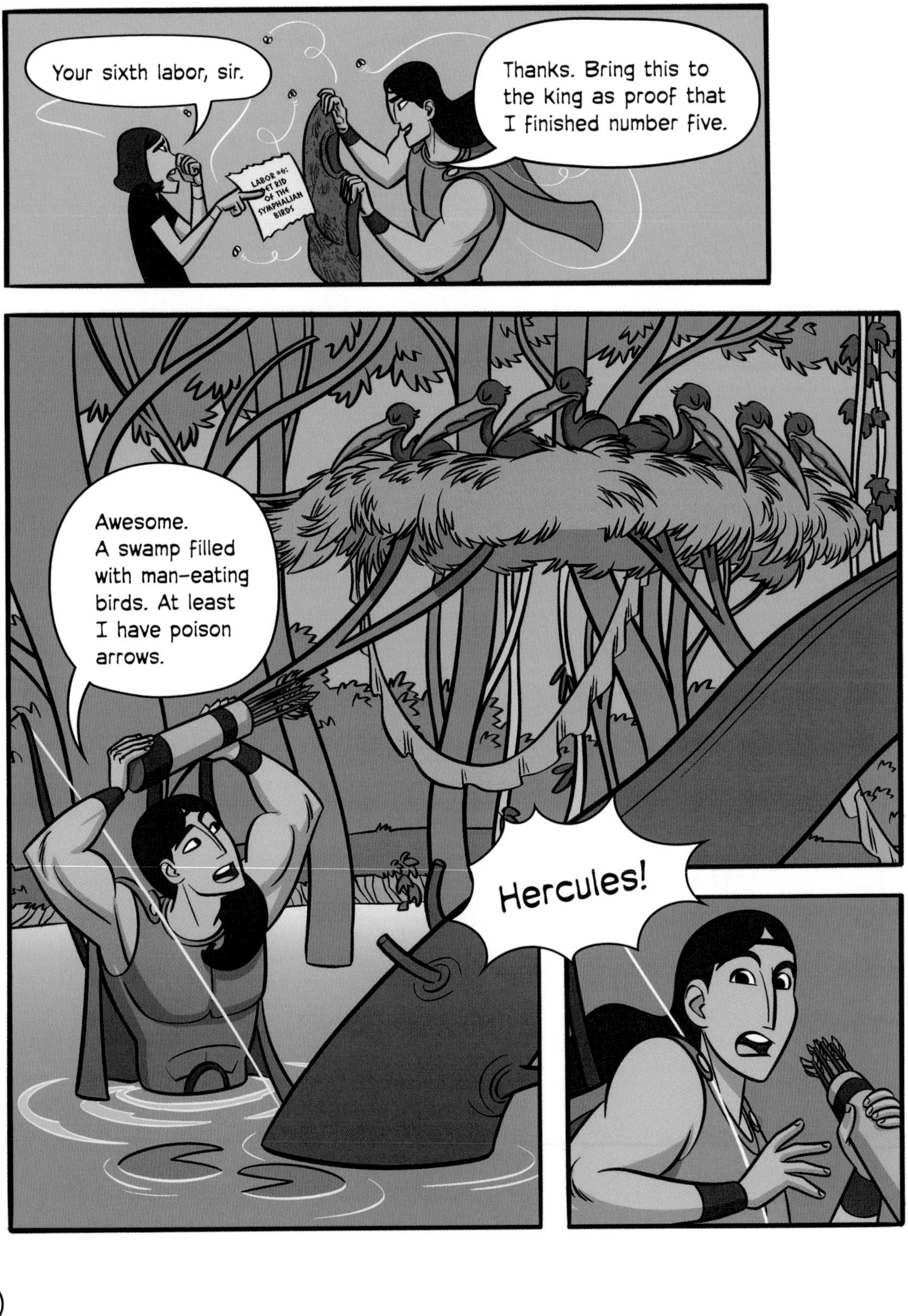
Your sixth labor, sir.
LABOR #6: ET RID OF THE SYMPHALIAN BIRDS
Thanks. Bring this to the king as proof that I finished number five.
Awesome. A swamp filled with man-eating birds. At least I have poison arrows.
Hercules!

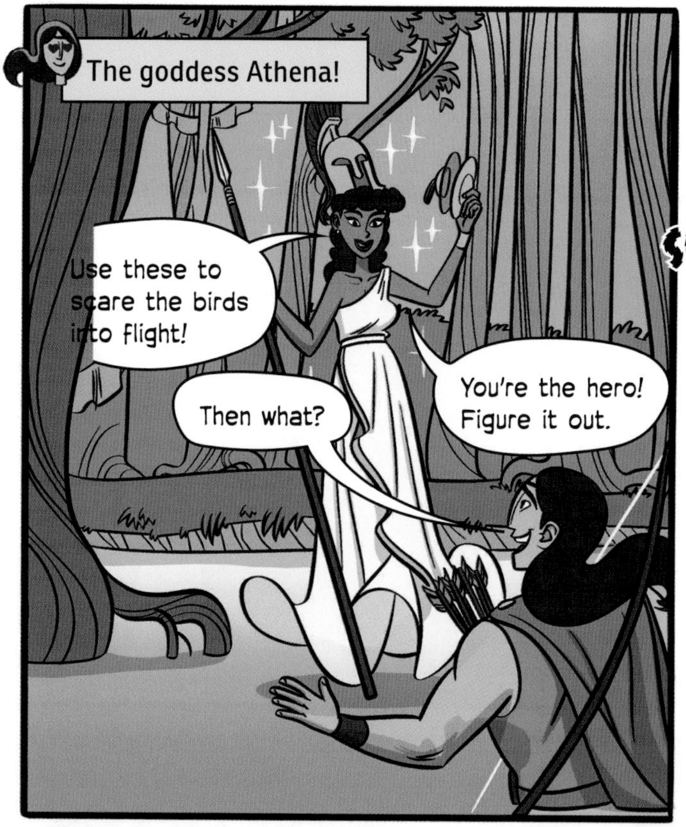
The goddess Athena!
Use these to scare the birds into flight!
Then what?
You're the hero! Figure it out.

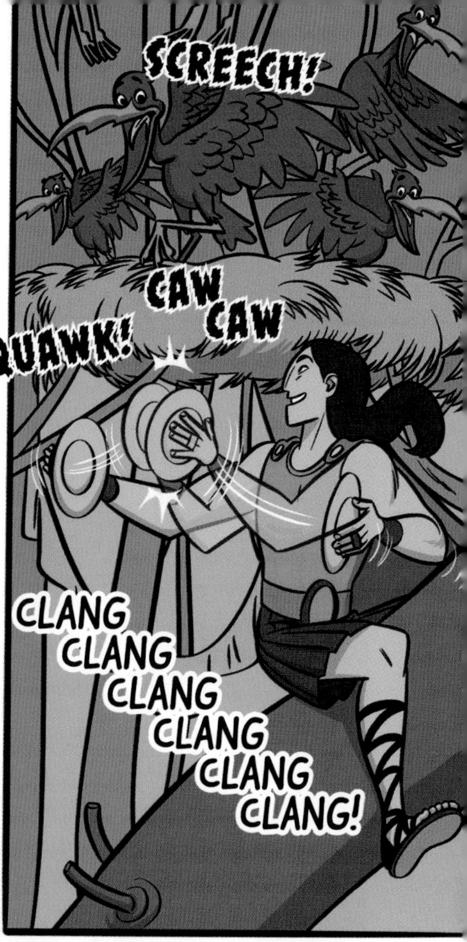
SCREECH!
CAW CAW
SQUAWK!
CLANG CLANG CLANG CLANG CLANG CLANG!

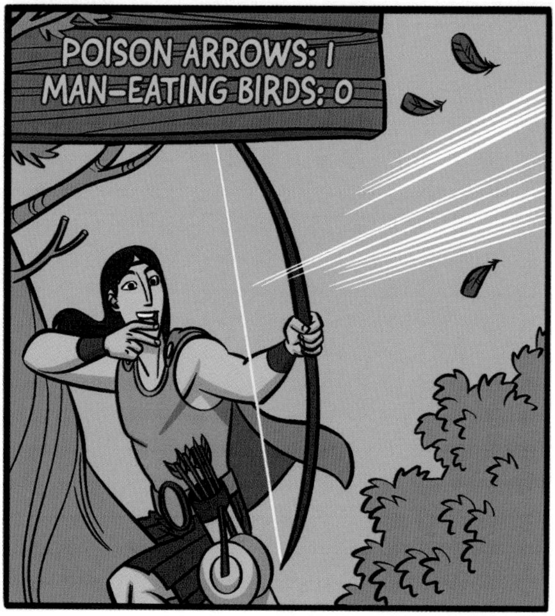
POISON ARROWS: 1
MAN-EATING BIRDS: 0

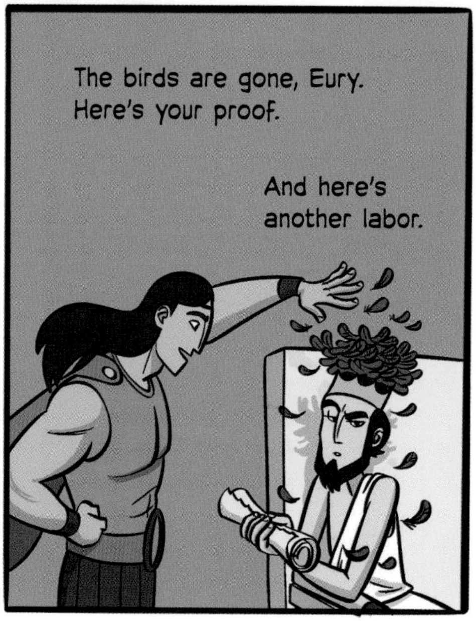
The birds are gone, Eury. Here's your proof.
And here's another labor.

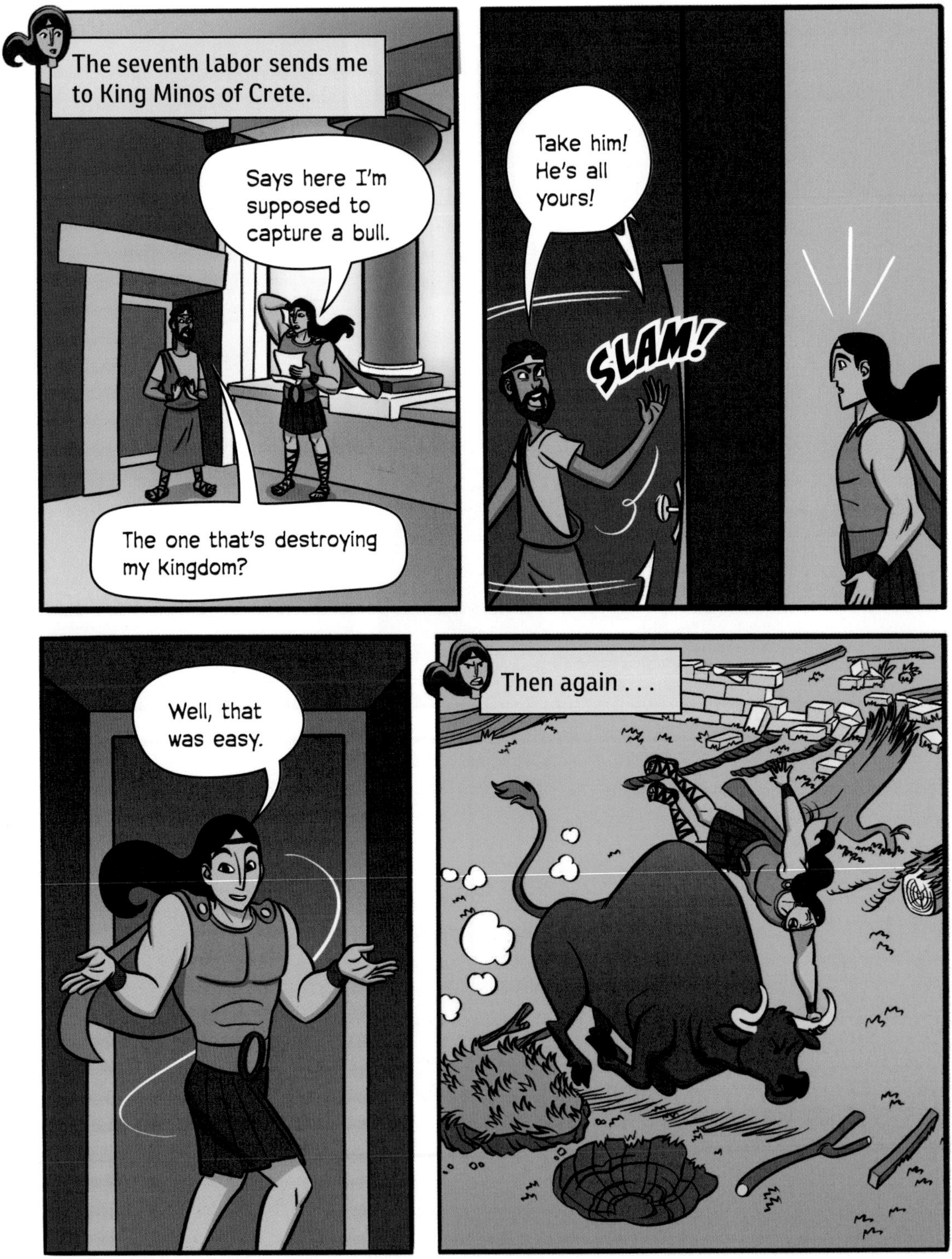
The seventh labor sends me to King Minos of Crete.
Says here I'm supposed to capture a bull.
The one that's destroying my kingdom?
Take him! He's all yours!
SLAM!
Well, that was easy.
Then again . . .

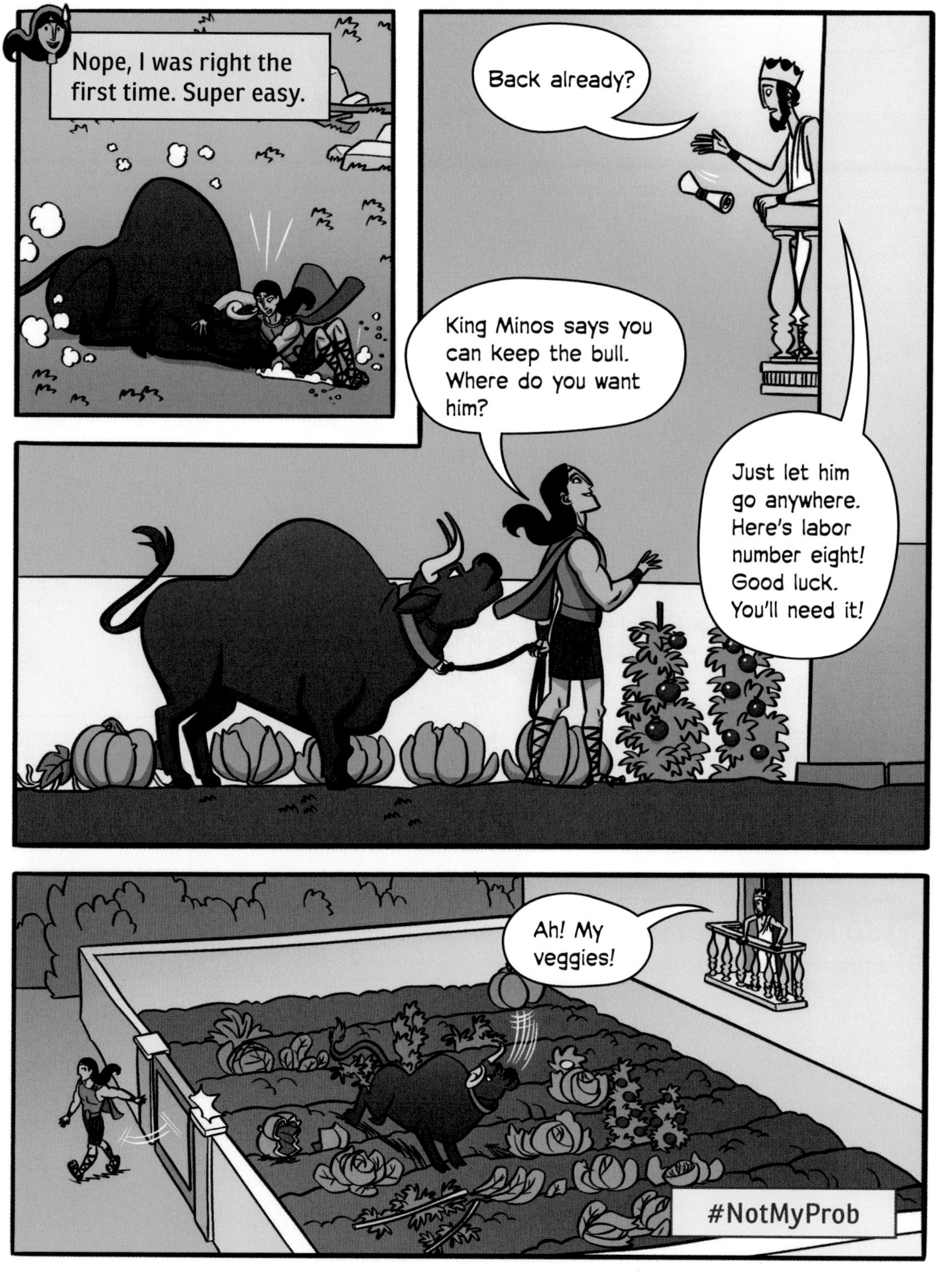
Nope, I was right the first time. Super easy.
Back already?
King Minos says you can keep the bull. Where do you want him?
Just let him go anywhere. Here's labor number eight! Good luck. You'll need it!
Ah! My veggies!
#NotMyProb

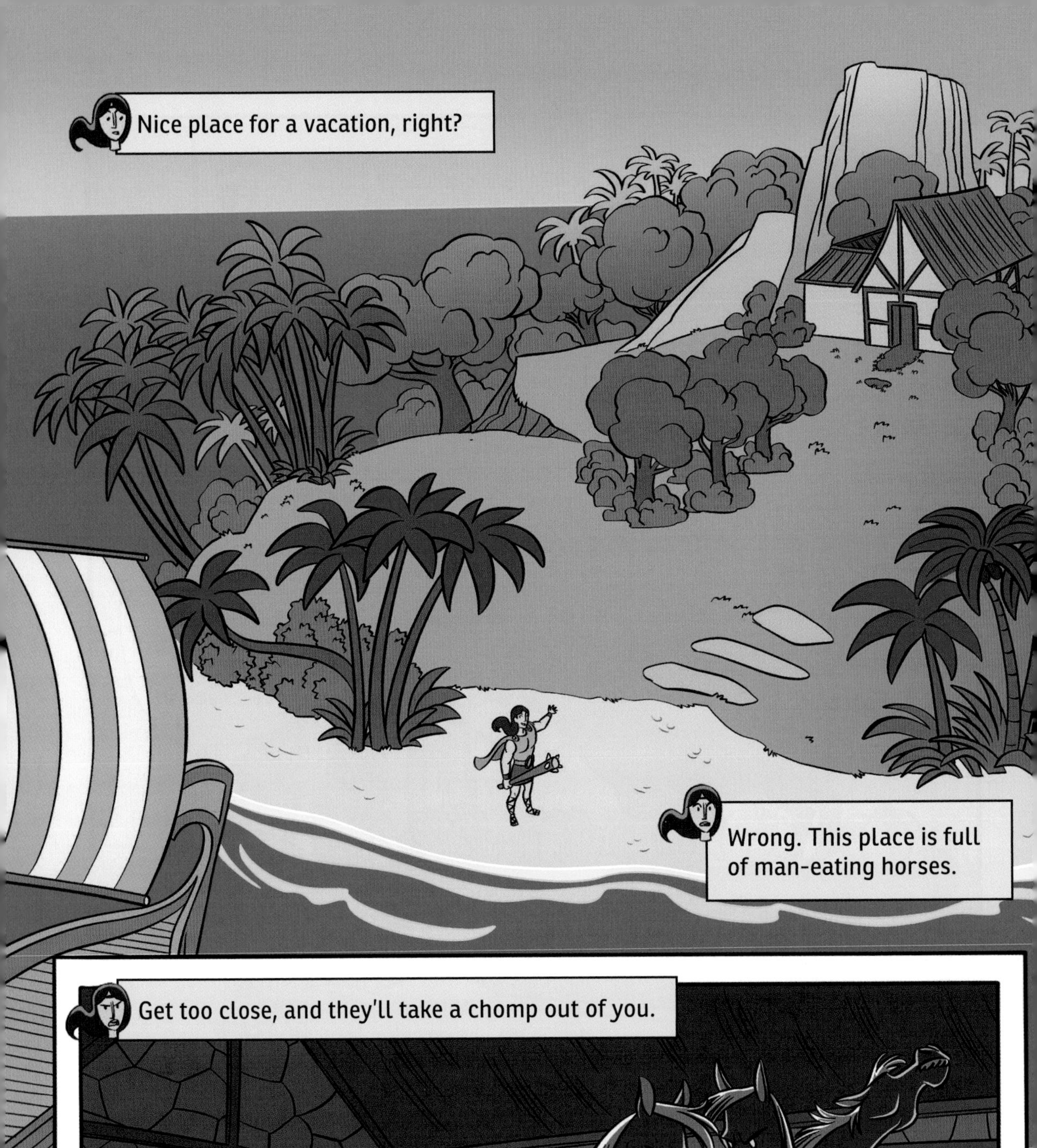
Nice place for a vacation, right?
Wrong. This place is full of man-eating horses.
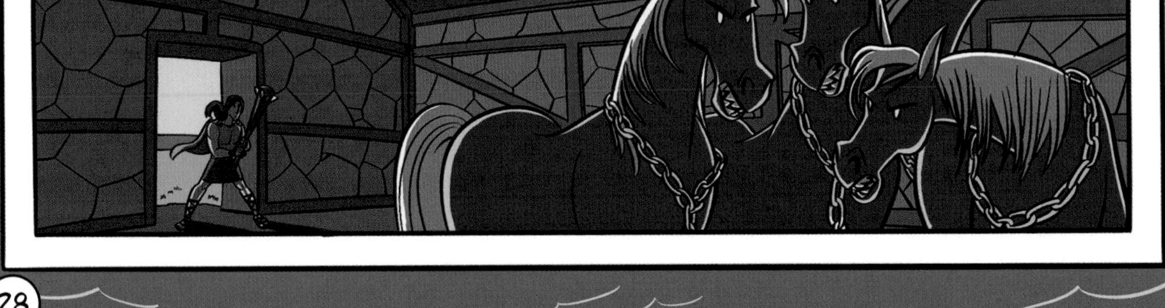
Get too close, and they'll take a chomp out of you.

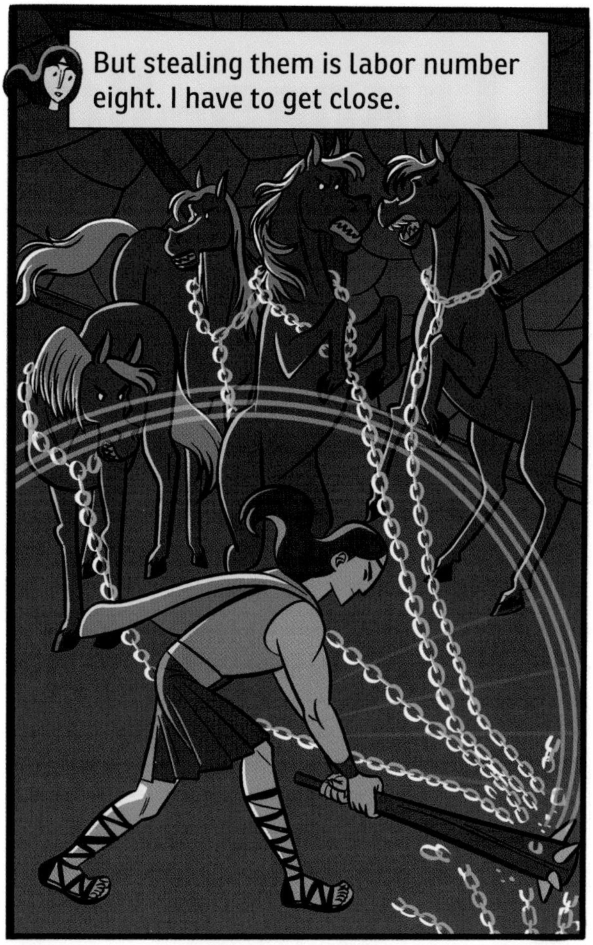
But stealing them is labor number eight. I have to get close.

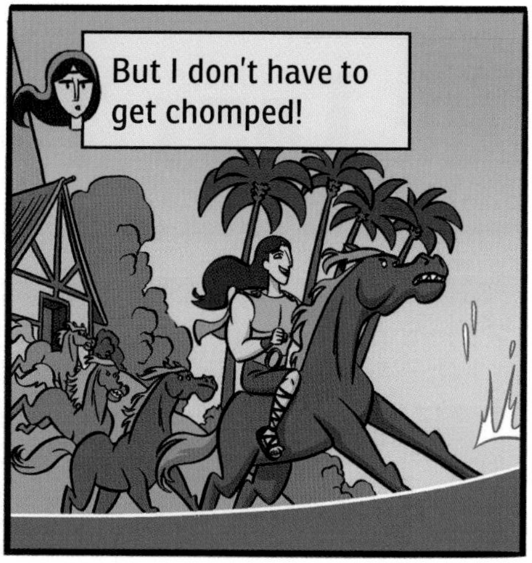
But I don't have to get chomped!

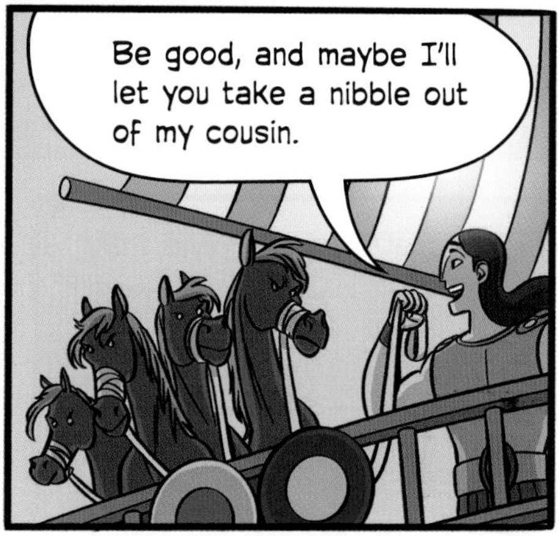
Be good, and maybe I'll let you take a nibble out of my cousin.

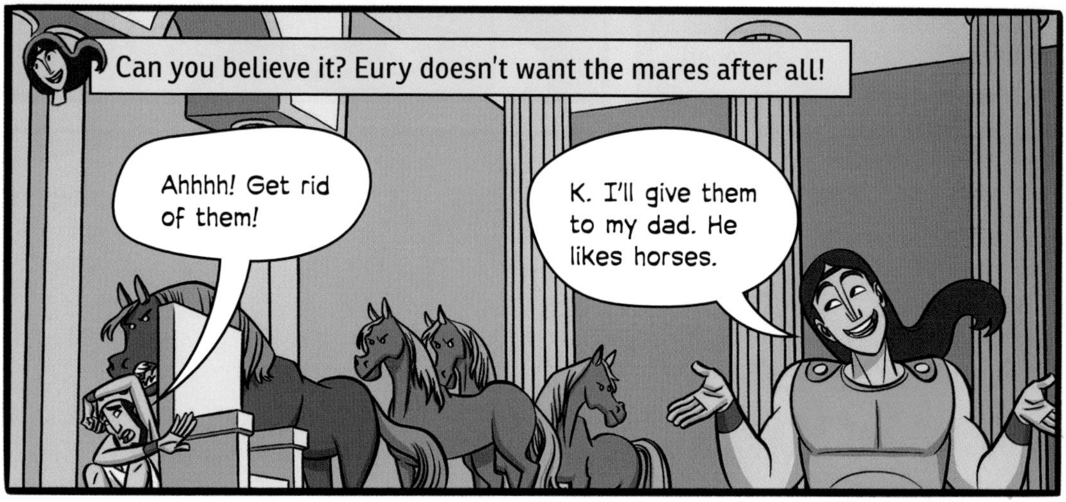
Can you believe it? Eury doesn't want the mares after all!
Ahhhh! Get rid of them!
K. I'll give them to my dad. He likes horses.

CHAPTER 4

THE LAST TWO LABORS—NOT!

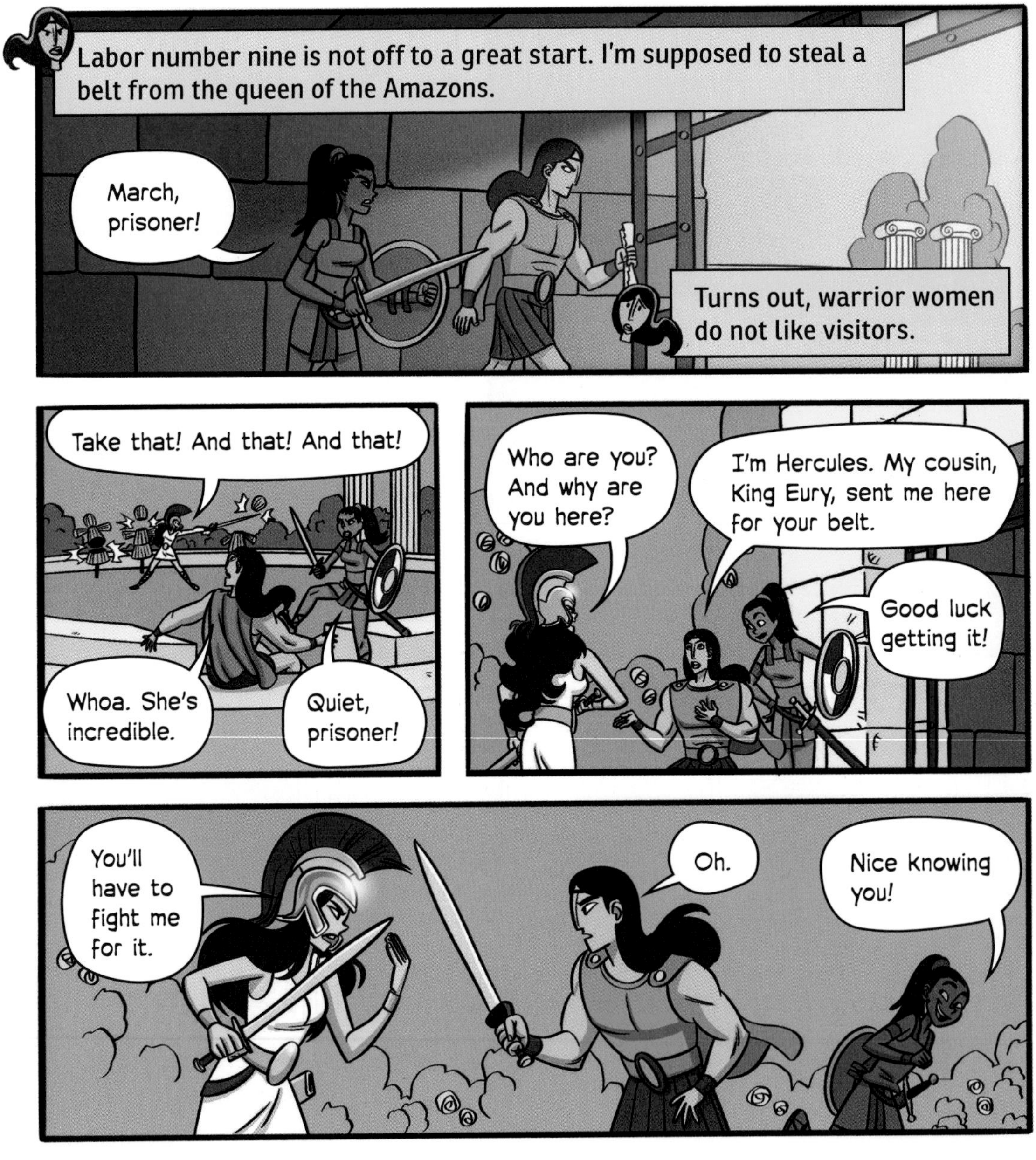

Labor number nine is not off to a great start. I'm supposed to steal a belt from the queen of the Amazons.
March, prisoner!
Turns out, warrior women do not like visitors.
Take that! And that! And that!
Whoa. She's incredible.
Quiet, prisoner!
Who are you? And why are you here?
I'm Hercules. My cousin, King Eury, sent me here for your belt.
Good luck getting it!
You'll have to fight me for it.
Oh.
Nice knowing you!

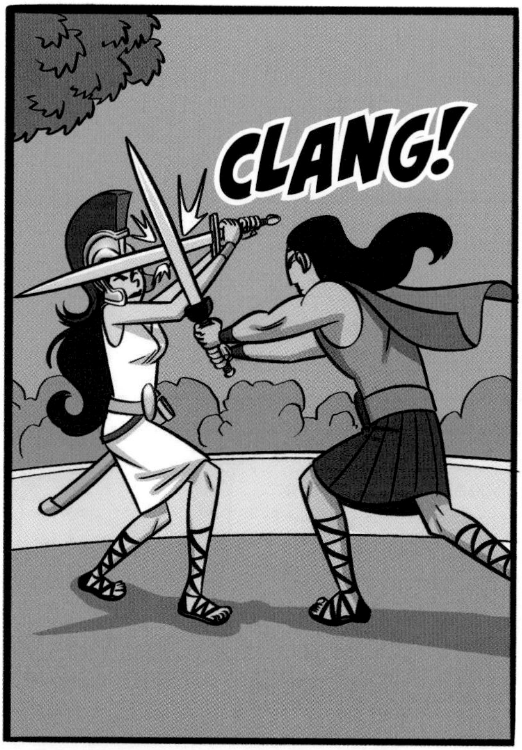
CLANG!
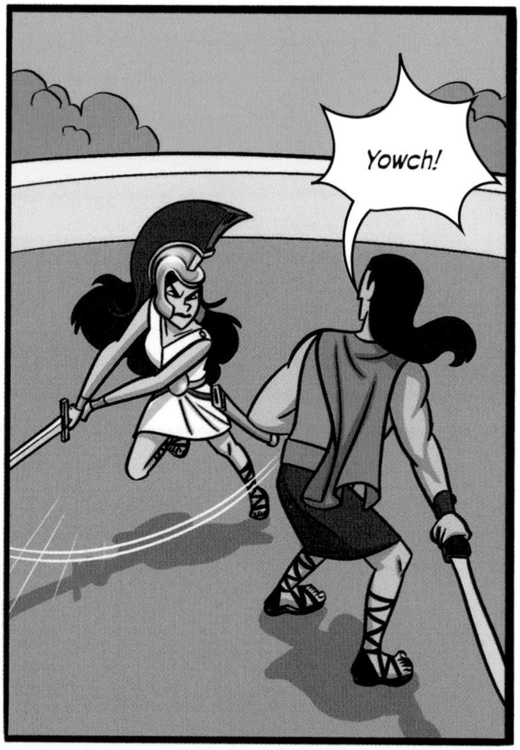
Yowch!
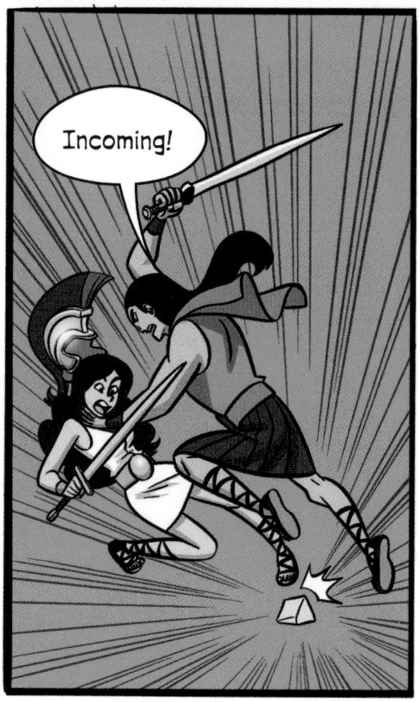
Incoming!
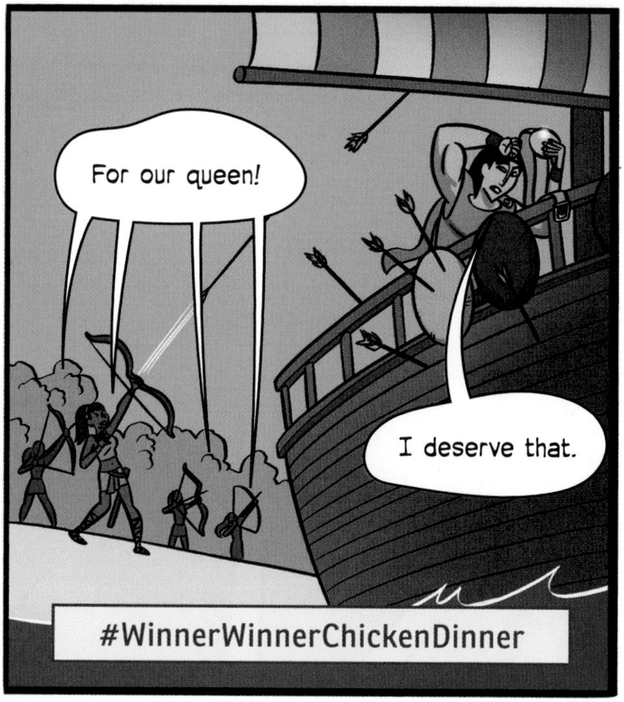
For our queen!
I deserve that.
#WinnerWinnerChickenDinner

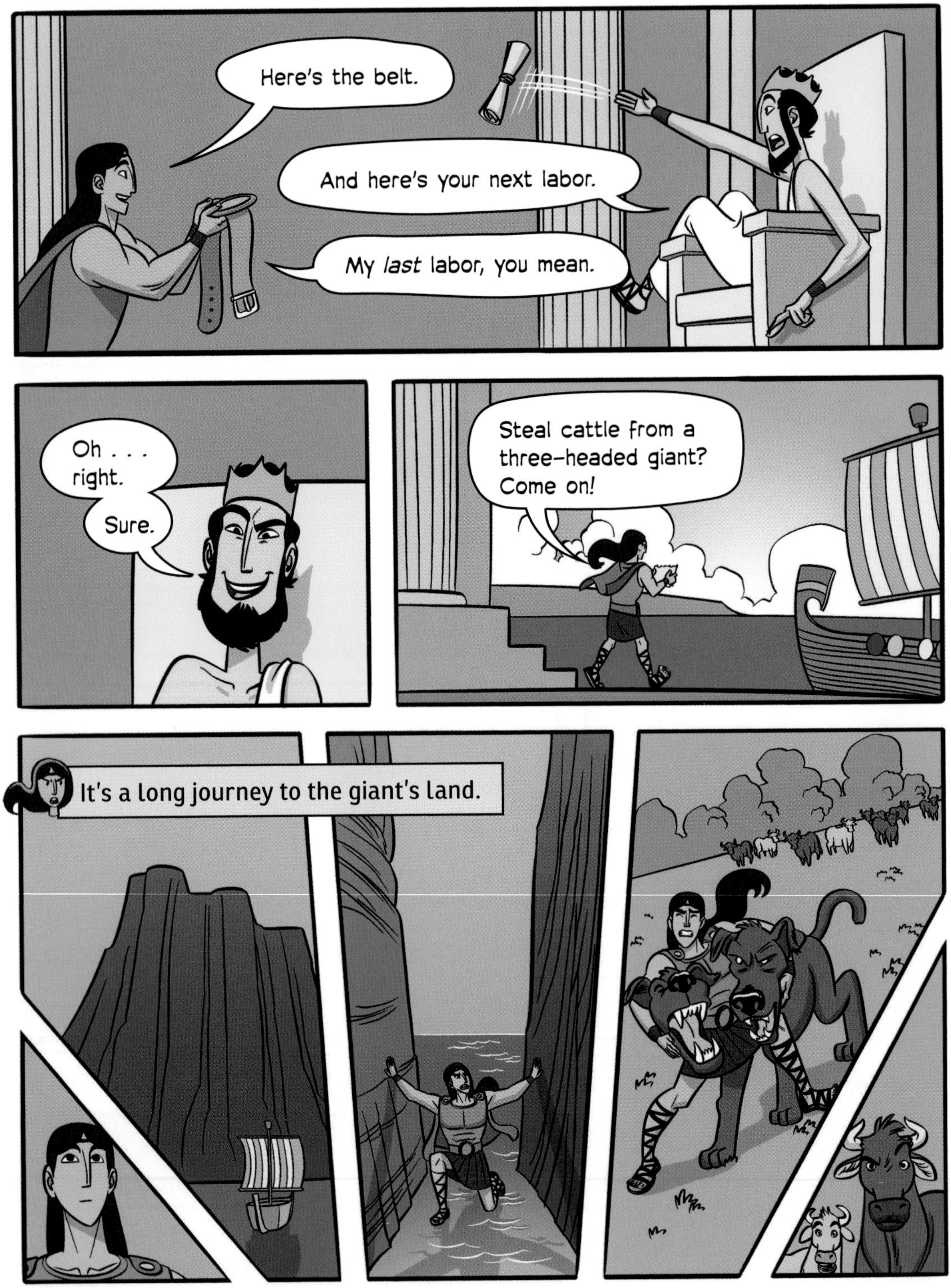

Here's the belt.
And here's your next labor.
My *last* labor, you mean.
Oh . . . right.
Sure.
Steal cattle from a three-headed giant? Come on!
It's a long journey to the giant's land.

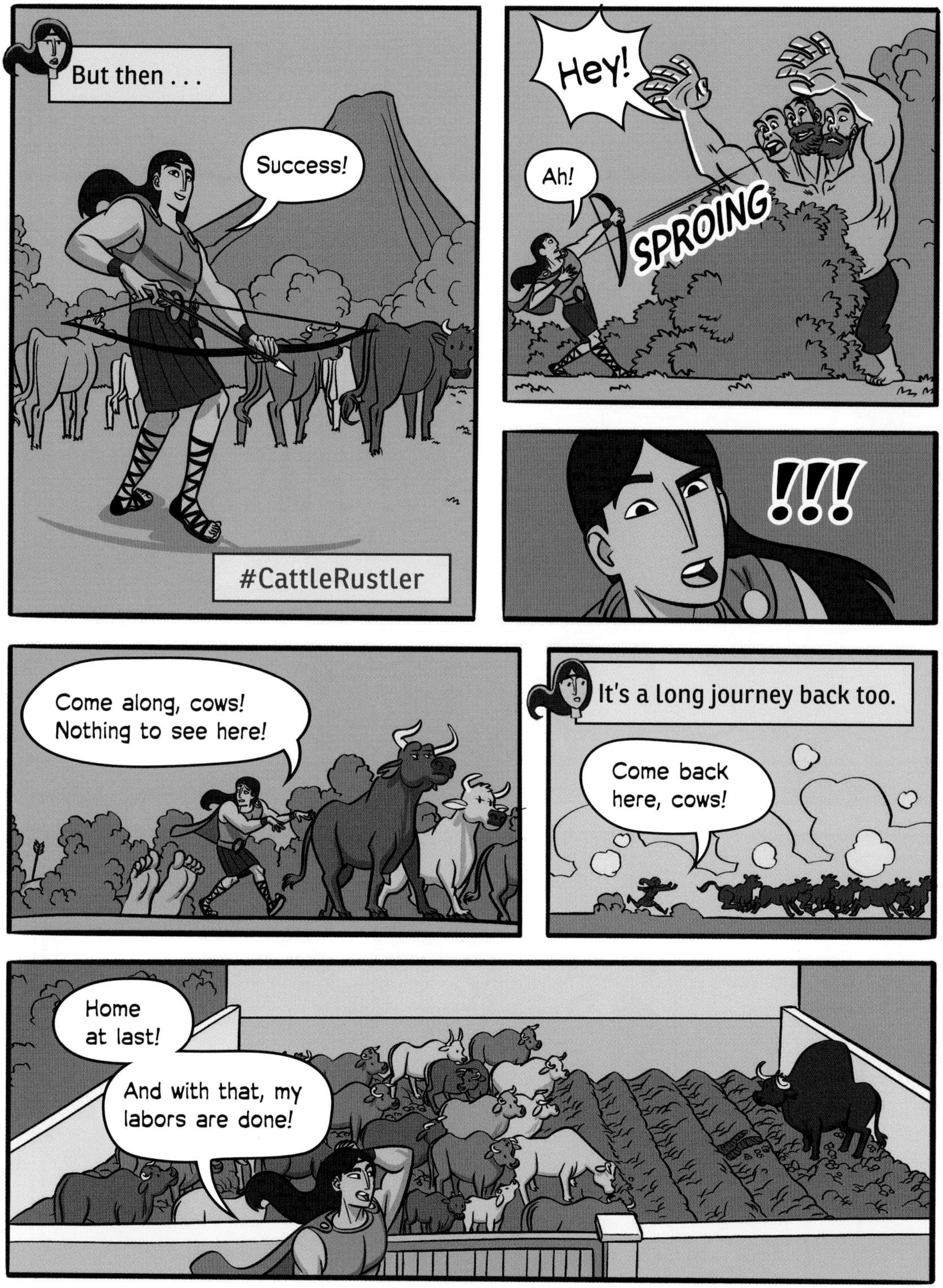
But then . . .
Success!
#CattleRustler
Hey!
Ah!
SPROING
!!!
Come along, cows! Nothing to see here!
It's a long journey back too.
Come back here, cows!
Home at last!
And with that, my labors are done!

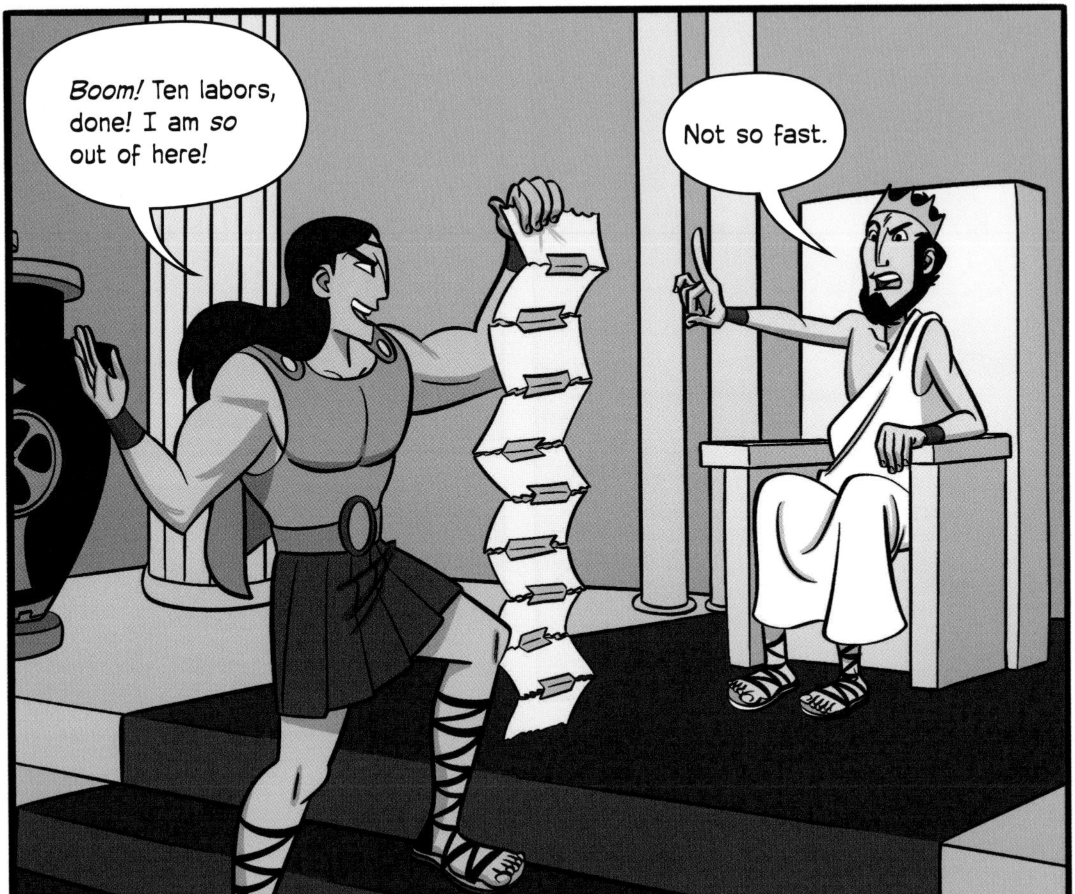
Boom! Ten labors, done! I am *so* out of here!
Not so fast.

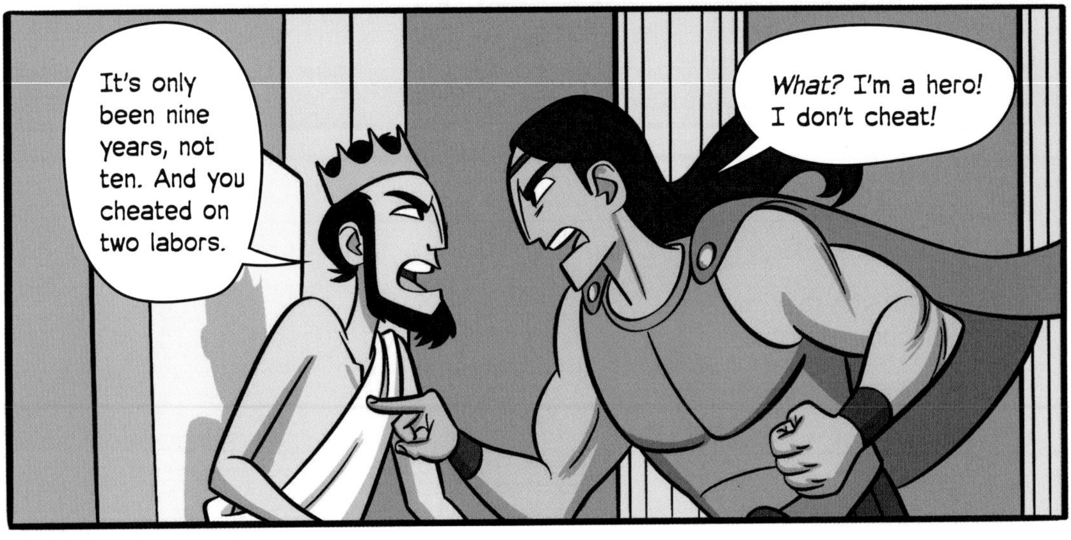
It's only been nine years, not ten. And you cheated on two labors.
What? I'm a hero! I don't cheat!

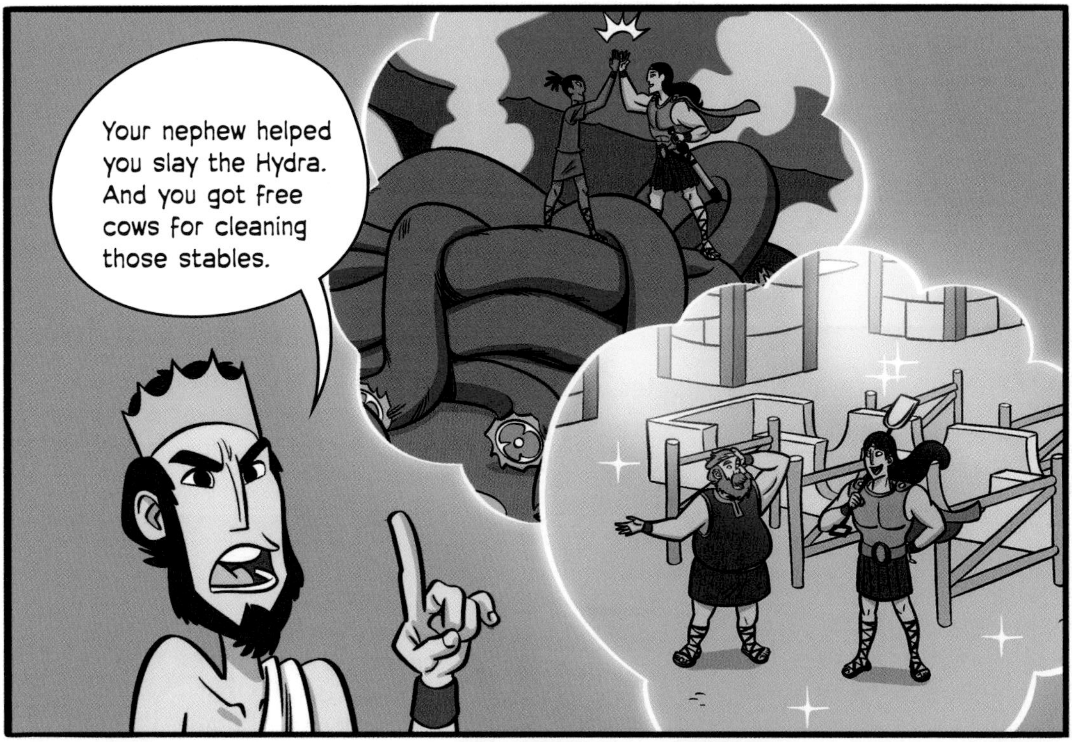
Your nephew helped you slay the Hydra. And you got free cows for cleaning those stables.

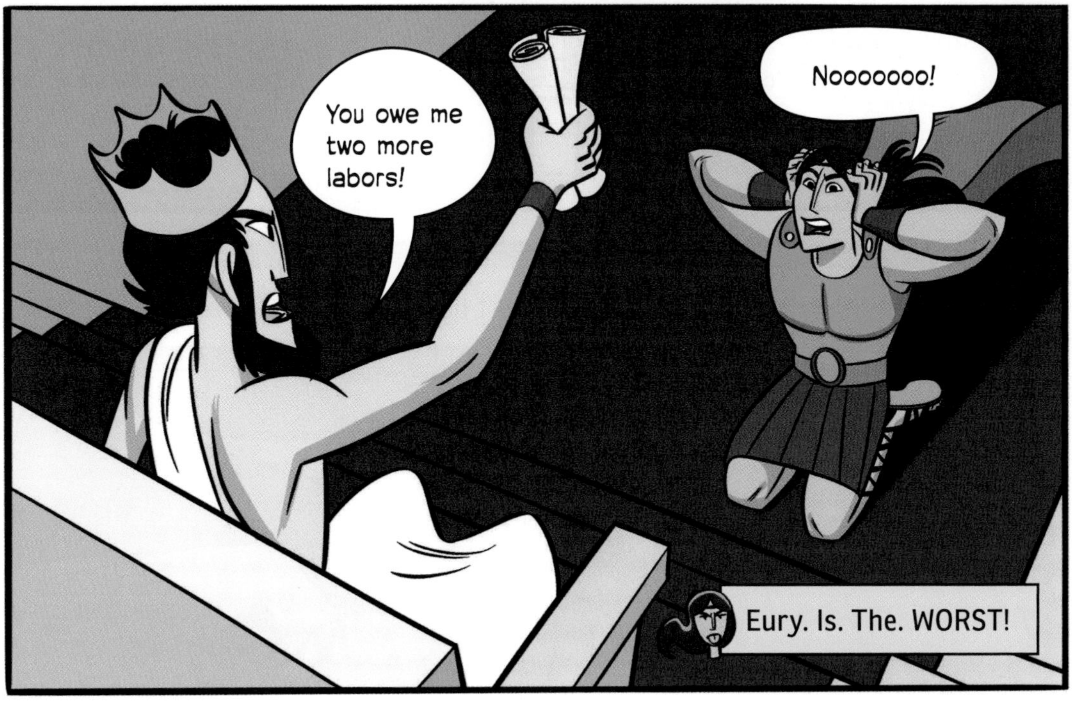
You owe me two more labors!
Nooooooo!
Eury. Is. The. WORST!

CHAPTER 5

The Last Two Labors (For Real This Time!)

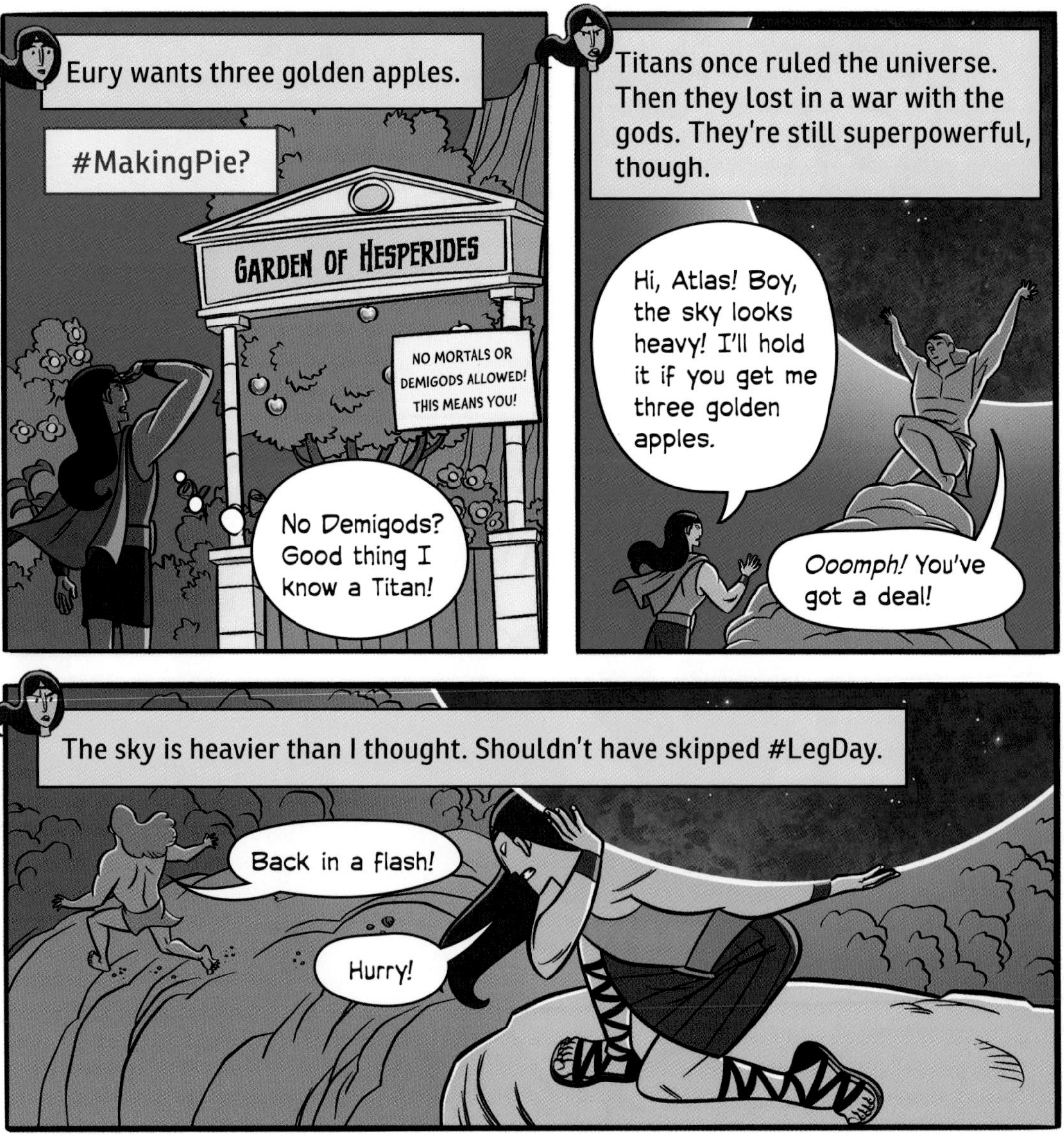
Eury wants three golden apples.
#MakingPie?
GARDEN OF HESPERIDES
NO MORTALS OR DEMIGODS ALLOWED! THIS MEANS YOU!
No Demigods? Good thing I know a Titan!
Titans once ruled the universe. Then they lost in a war with the gods. They're still superpowerful, though.
Hi, Atlas! Boy, the sky looks heavy! I'll hold it if you get me three golden apples.
Ooomph! You've got a deal!
The sky is heavier than I thought. Shouldn't have skipped #LegDay.
Back in a flash!
Hurry!

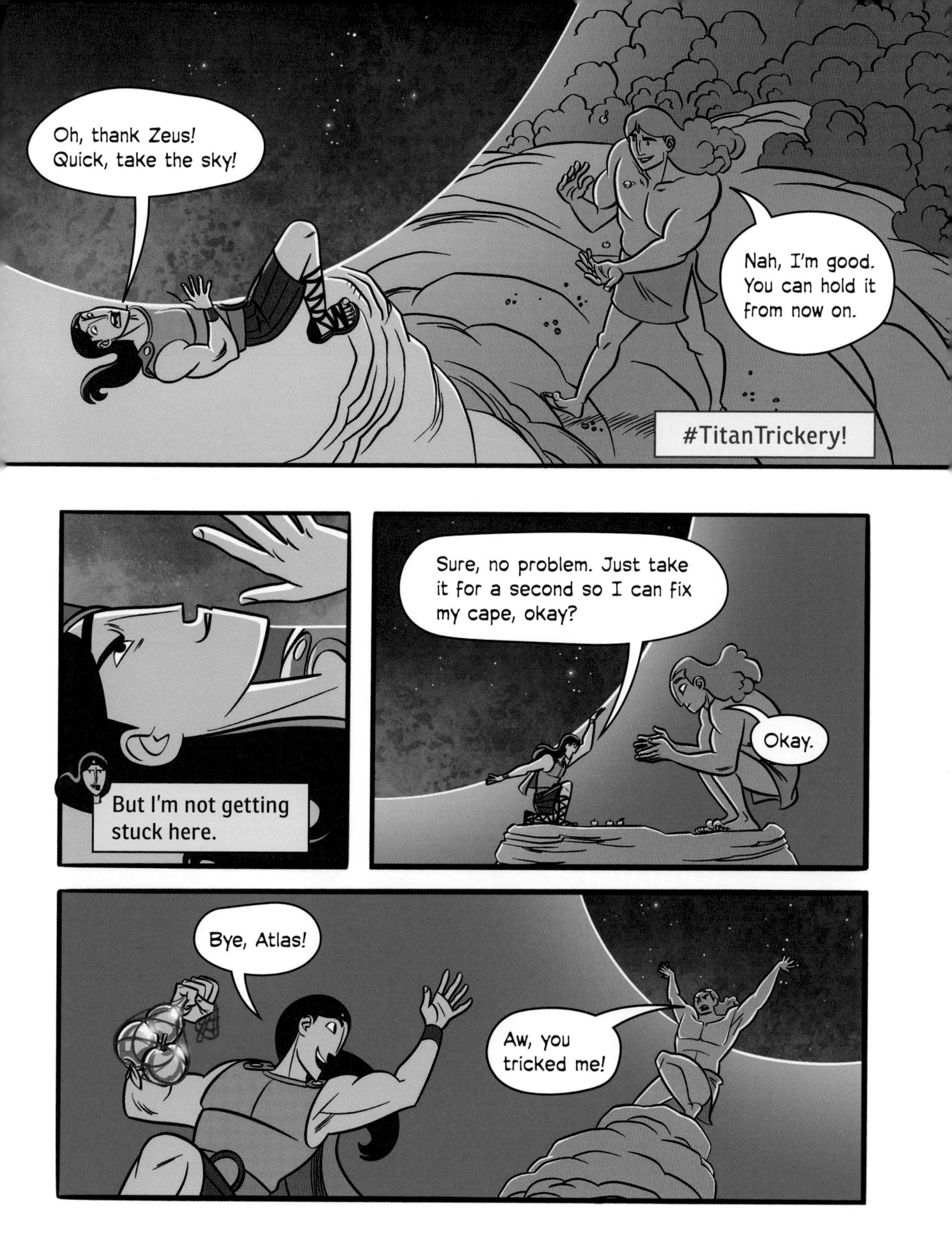
Oh, thank Zeus! Quick, take the sky!
Nah, I'm good. You can hold it from now on.
#TitanTrickery!
But I'm not getting stuck here.
Sure, no problem. Just take it for a second so I can fix my cape, okay?
Okay.
Bye, Atlas!
Aw, you tricked me!

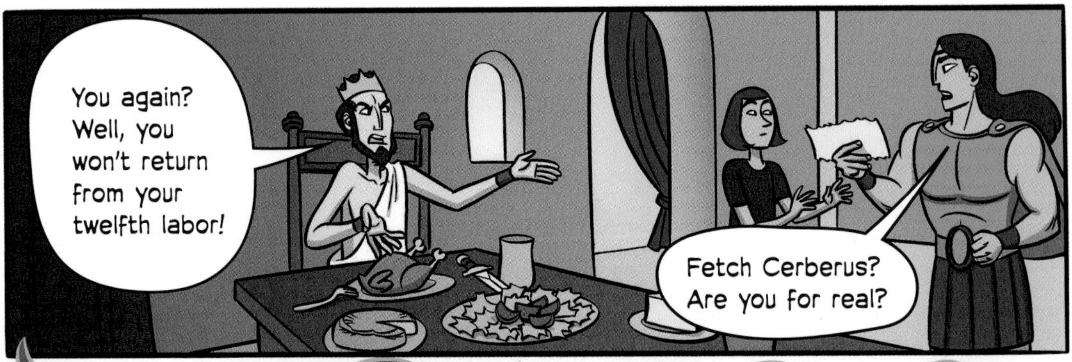
You again? Well, you won't return from your twelfth labor!
Fetch Cerberus? Are you for real?

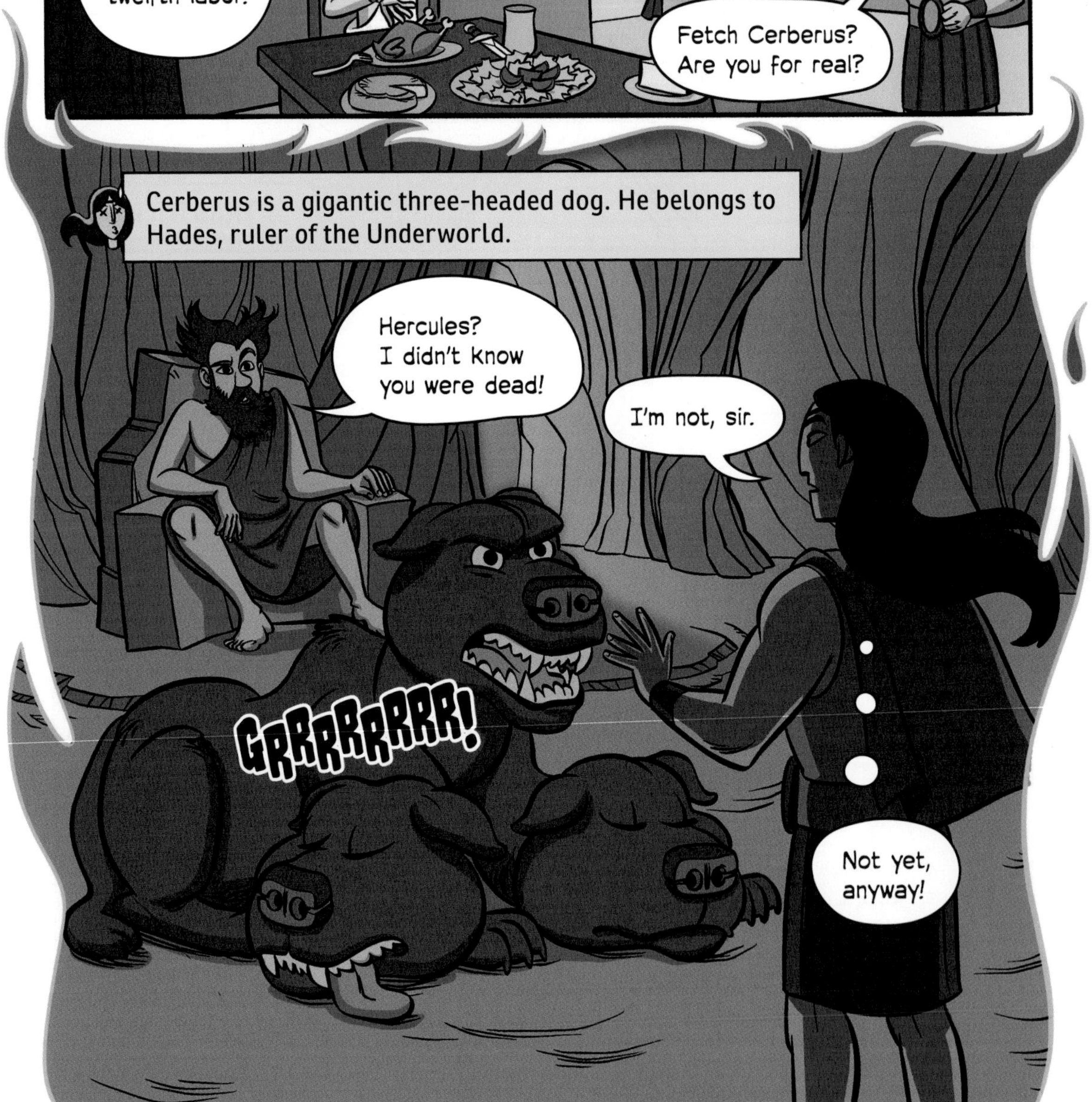
Cerberus is a gigantic three-headed dog. He belongs to Hades, ruler of the Underworld.
Hercules? I didn't know you were dead!
I'm not, sir.
GRRRRRRRR!
Not yet, anyway!

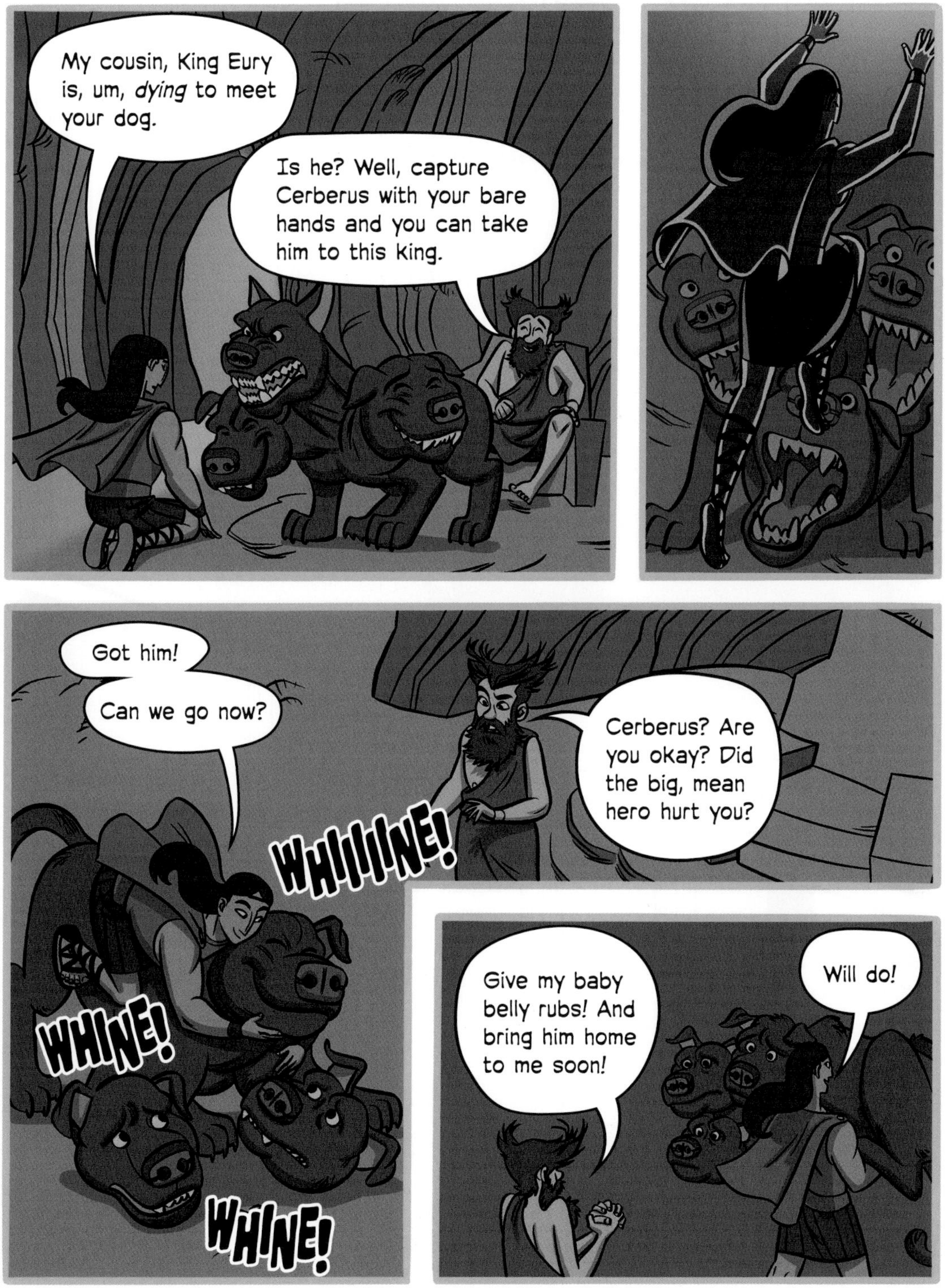
My cousin, King Eury is, um, *dying* to meet your dog.
Is he? Well, capture Cerberus with your bare hands and you can take him to this king.
Got him!
Can we go now?
WHIIIINE!
Cerberus? Are you okay? Did the big, mean hero hurt you?
WHINE!
WHINE!
Give my baby belly rubs! And bring him home to me soon!
Will do!

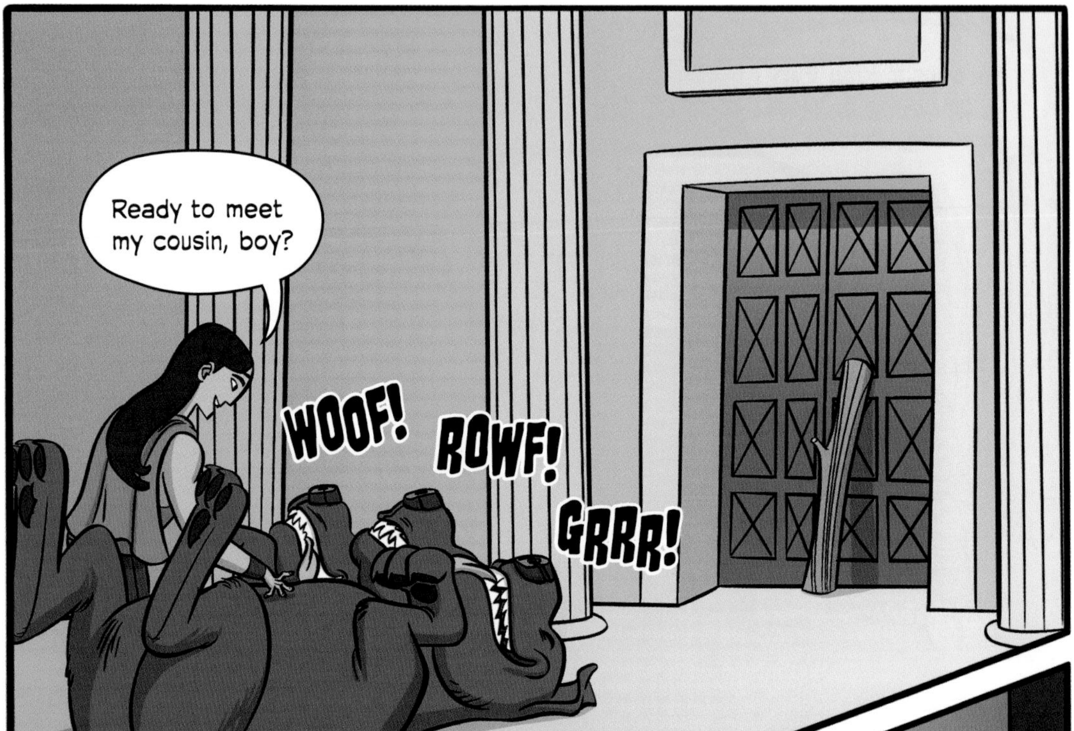
Ready to meet my cousin, boy?
WOOF!
ROWF!
GRRR!

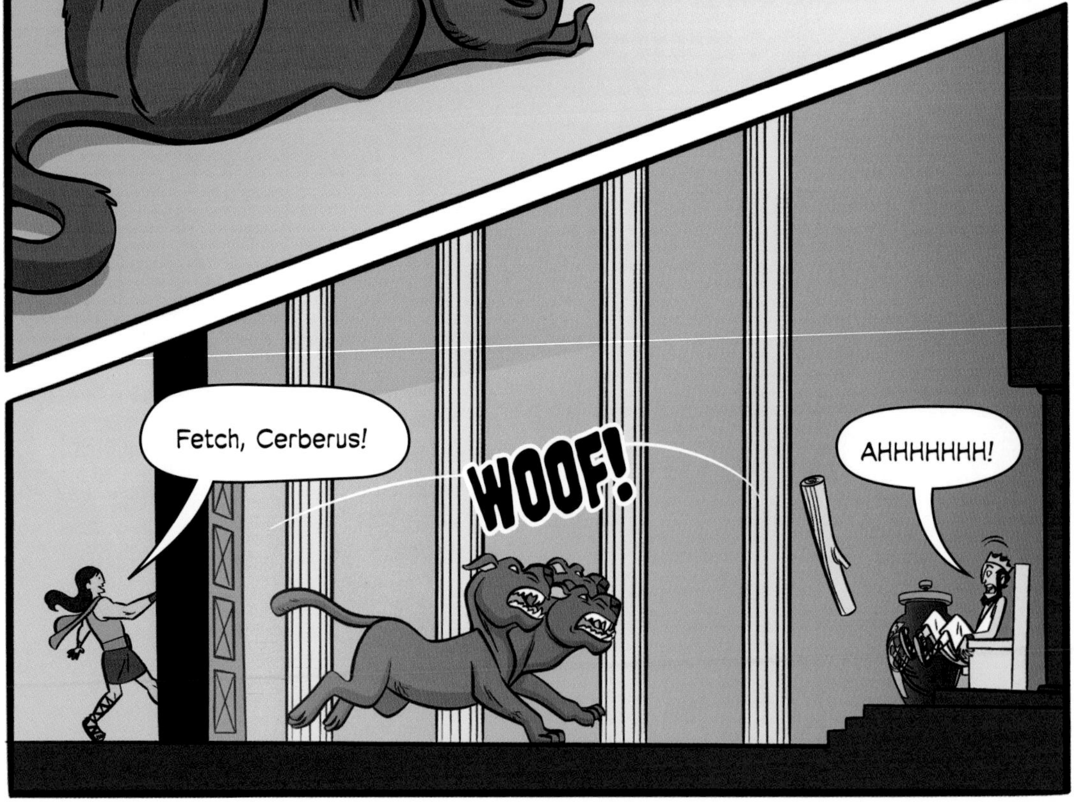
Fetch, Cerberus!
WOOF!
AHHHHHHH!

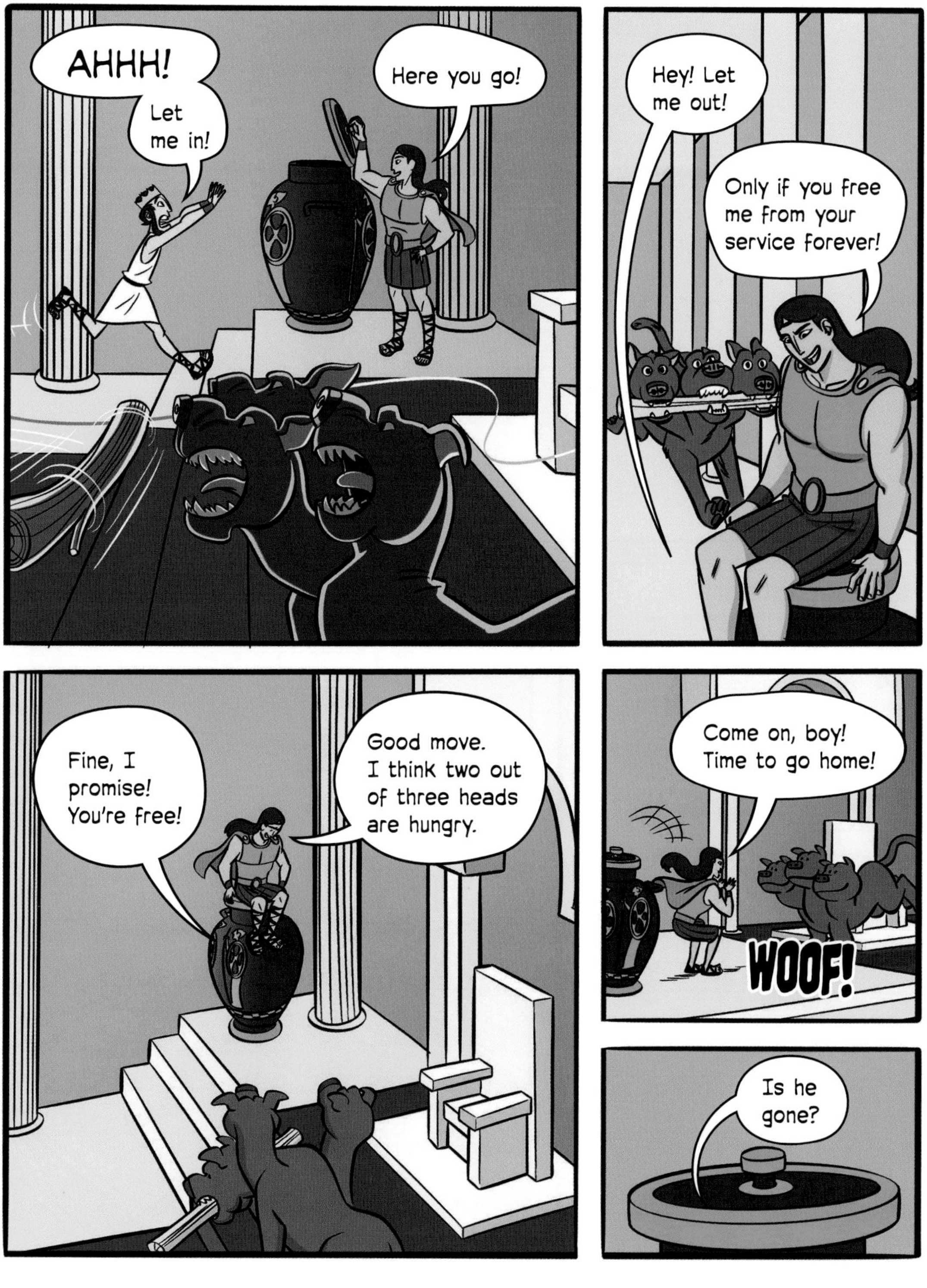
AHHH!
Let me in!
Here you go!
Hey! Let me out!
Only if you free me from your service forever!
Fine, I promise! You're free!
Good move. I think two out of three heads are hungry.
Come on, boy! Time to go home!
WOOF!
Is he gone?

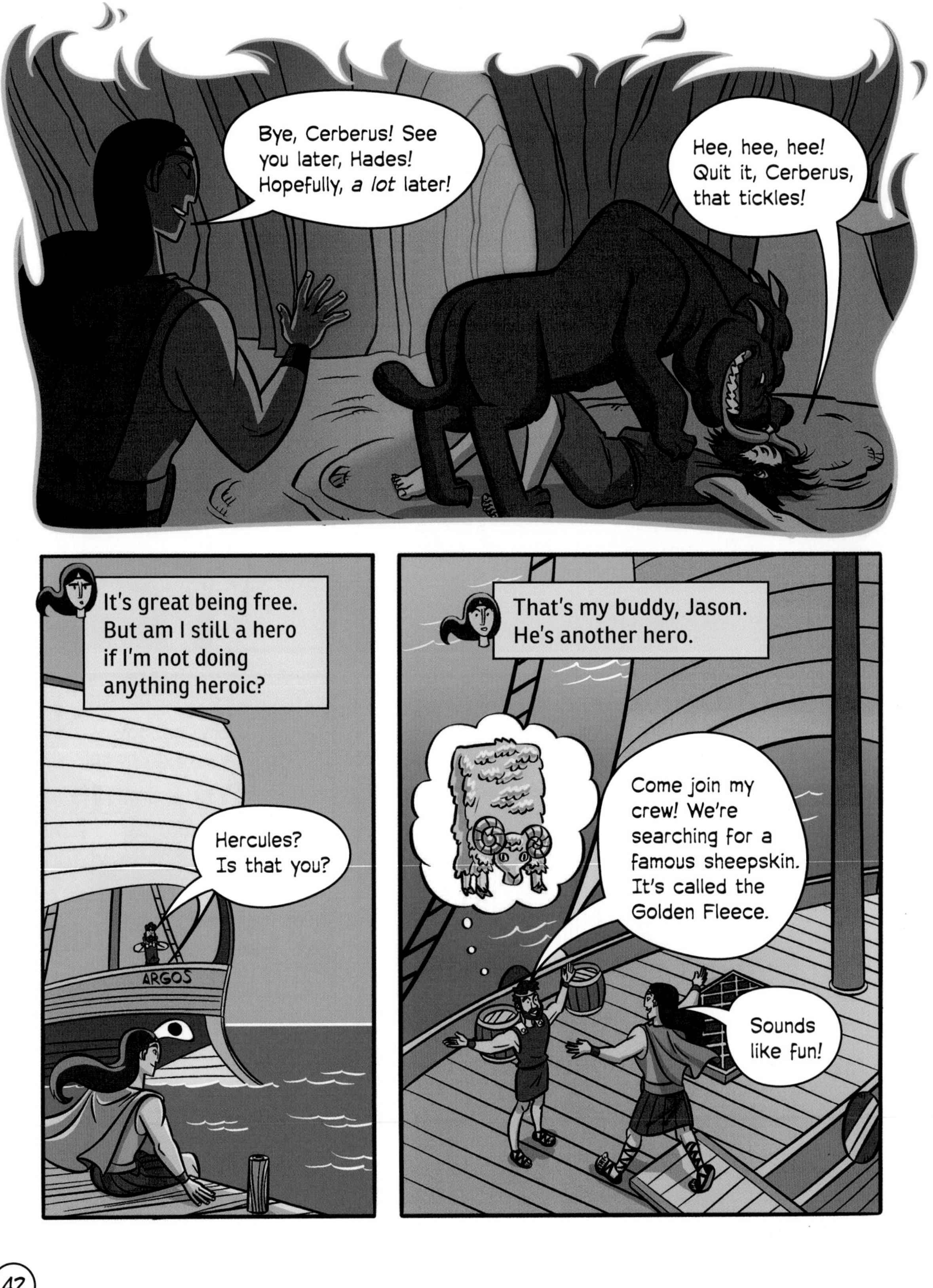
Bye, Cerberus! See you later, Hades! Hopefully, *a lot* later!
Hee, hee, hee! Quit it, Cerberus, that tickles!
It's great being free. But am I still a hero if I'm not doing anything heroic?
ARGOS
Hercules? Is that you?
That's my buddy, Jason. He's another hero.
Come join my crew! We're searching for a famous sheepskin. It's called the Golden Fleece.
Sounds like fun!

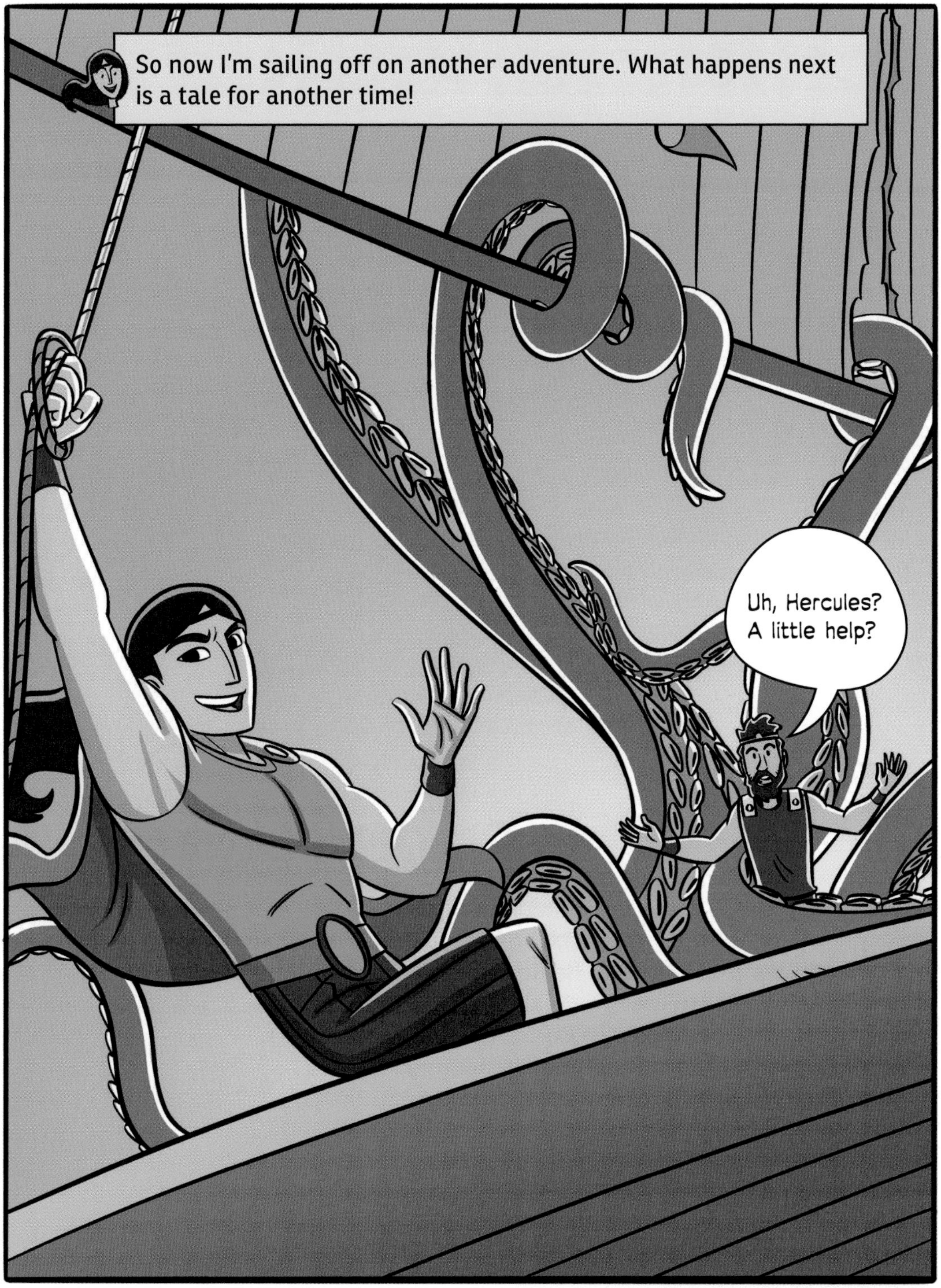
So now I'm sailing off on another adventure. What happens next is a tale for another time!
Uh, Hercules? A little help?

MORE ABOUT HERCULES

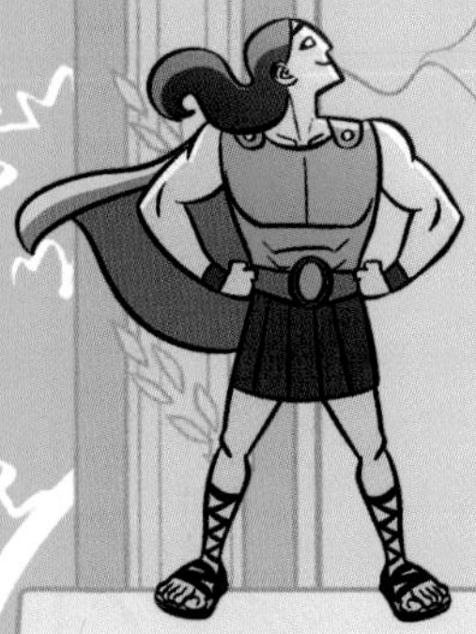

Hercules is also known by other names. His original Greek name was Herakles or Heracles.

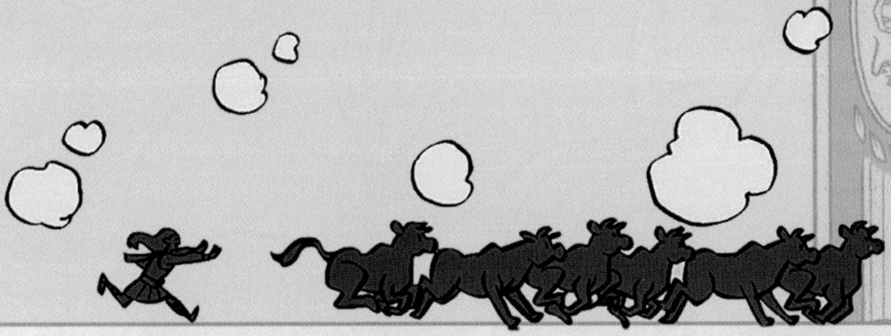

Hercules was a great fighter. On his way home with the cattle, he defeated a fire-breathing giant named Cacus. That wasn't part of his labors, just a side adventure!

Hercules was so famous that his image was featured on one of the first Roman coins ever made.

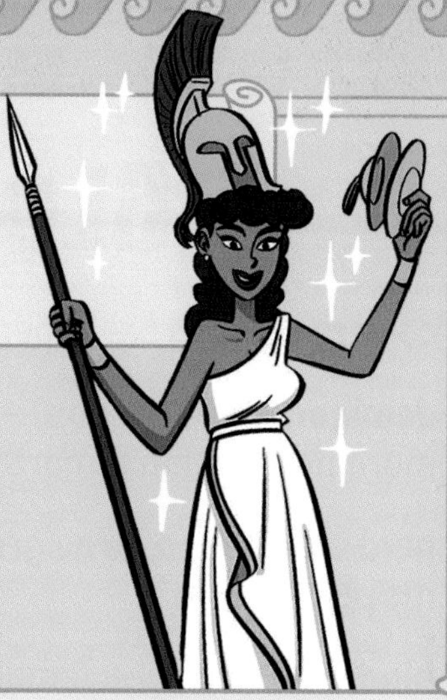

Hercules and a river god once fought to win the hand of a beautiful woman. Hercules won. That same woman almost killed Hercules by wrapping him in a robe soaked in poison! The goddess Athena saved him.

No one knows for sure if Hercules was a real man. But tales of his heroic adventures have lived on for thousands of years.

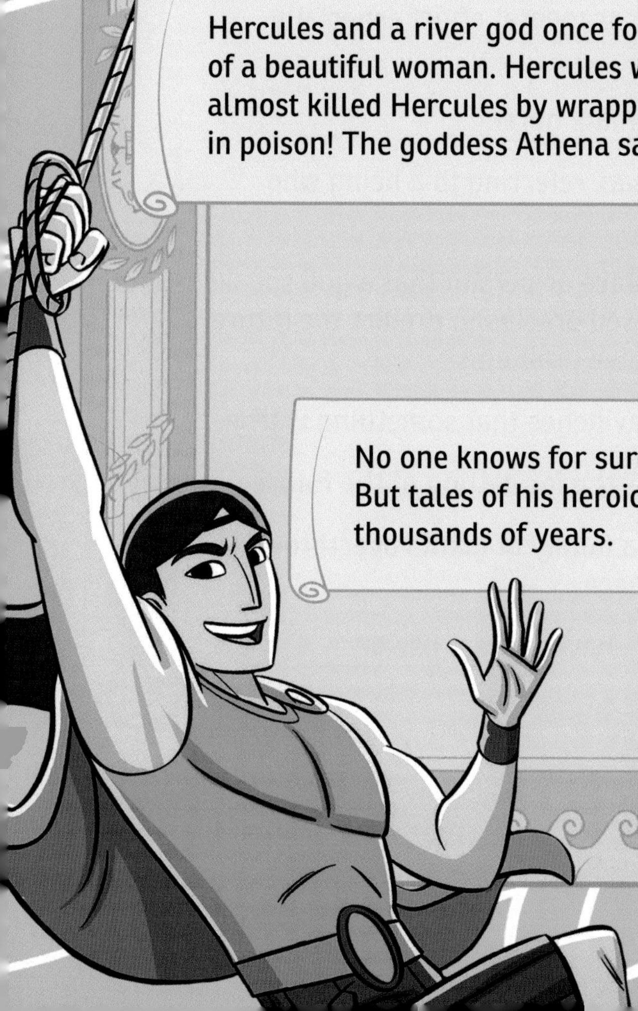

Glossary

coward (KOU-erd)—a person who shows shameful fear

demigod (DEM-ee-god)—a mythological being with more power than a mortal but less than a god

herd (HURD)—a large group of animals that lives or moves together

hind (HAHYND)—a female deer

labor (LEY-ber)—physical or mental effort especially when hard or required

mare (MAIR)—an adult female horse

mortal (MOR-tuhl)—human, referring to a being who will eventually die

oracle (OR-uh-kuhl)—a place or person that a god speaks through; in myths, gods used oracles to predict the future or to tell people how to solve problems

proof (PROOF)—facts or evidence that something is true

prophecy (PROF-uh-see)—the foretelling of the future

Titan (TAHYT-n)—one of a family of giants overthrown by the gods of ancient Greece

valuable (VAL-yoo-buhl)—having great use or importance

INTERNET SITES

Ancient Greek Gods for Kids: The 12 Labors of Hercules
greece.mrdonn.org/greekgods/hercules.html

Kids Love Greece: The 12 Labors of Hercules
kidslovegreece.com/greece_online/the-12-labors-of-hercules

Stories to Grow By: Hercules (Heracles) and His Labors
storiestogrowby.org/story/hercules-heracles-labors-greek-myth-story

---

OTHER BOOKS IN THIS SERIES

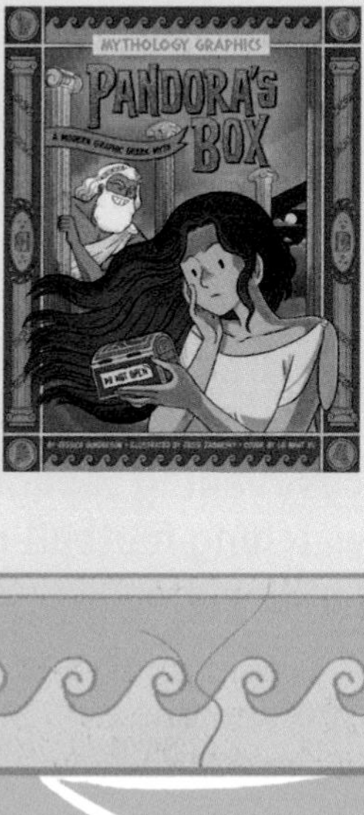
MYTHOLOGY GRAPHICS
PANDORA'S BOX

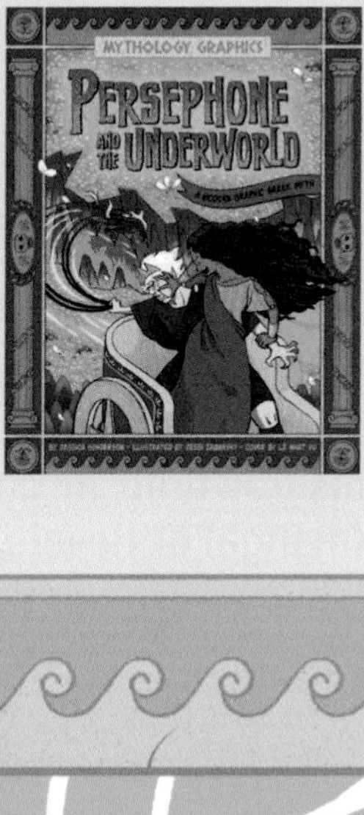
MYTHOLOGY GRAPHICS
PERSEPHONE AND THE UNDERWORLD

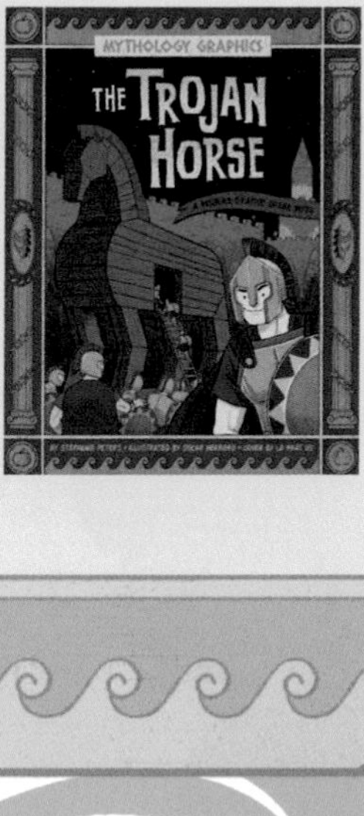
MYTHOLOGY GRAPHICS
THE TROJAN HORSE

ABOUT THE CREATORS

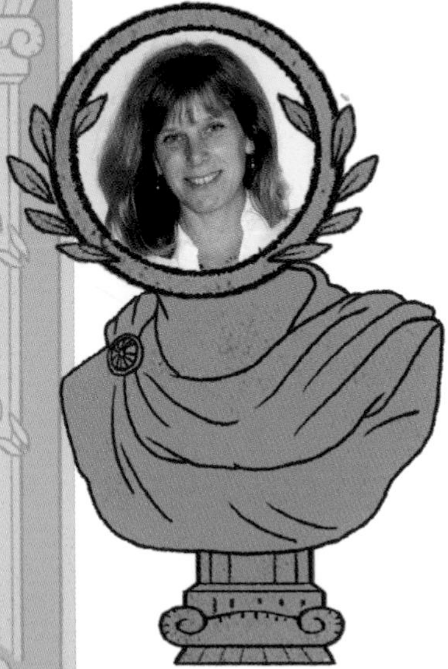

Stephanie Peters has been writing books for children for more than twenty-five years. Her most recent Capstone titles include *Earth's Amazing Journey: From Pebbles to Continents* and *The Trojan Horse: A Modern Graphic Greek Myth* from the Mythology Graphics series. An avid reader, workout enthusiast, and beach wanderer, Stephanie enjoys spending time with her family and their pets. She lives and works in Mansfield, Massachusetts.
Photo Credit: Daniel Peters

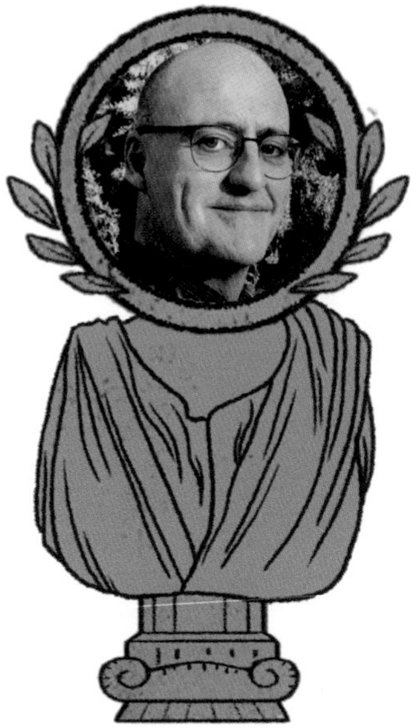

Oscar Herrero was born in Madrid, Spain, and studied journalism before deciding to devote himself entirely to art. He is an illustrator, character designer, and writer with experience illustrating children's books, comics, magazine covers, album cover art, and video games, as well as working as a visual development artist for leading animation studios.
Photo Credit: Diana Herrero

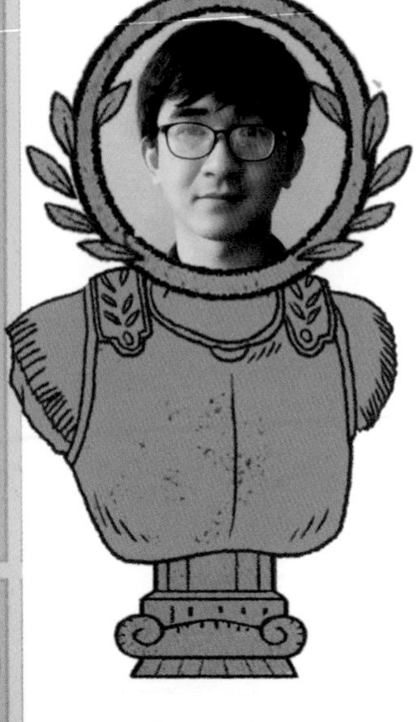

Le Nhat Vu was born in Nha Trang, a seaside city in Vietnam. He now works as a book illustrator in Ho Chi Minh City. He draws inspiration from fantasy, adventure, and poetic stories. During his free time, he enjoys reading Japanese comics (manga) or novels, watching football or movies—maybe with a cup of milk coffee.
Photo Credit: Le Nhat Vu